NEVER ALONE
A life of faith and total dependence on God

God has always been with me wherever I went.
To Him be all honour and glory.

By
João Garcia

Mill Lake Books

Copyright © 2020 by João Garcia
No part of this book may be reproduced in any form without written permission, except for brief quotations in critical reviews.

Published by Mill Lake Books
Abbotsford, BC
Canada

Unless otherwise noted, Scripture verses are taken from the NEW REVISED STANDARD VERSION BIBLE®, NRSV® Copyright © 1989 the Division of Christian Education of the National Council of the Churches of Christ in the United States of America Used by permission. All rights reserved.

Scripture verses designated GNT are taken from the Good News Translation Copyright © 1992 by American Bible Society.

ISBN: 978-1-7771926-0-0

Posthumous homage

to my parents

MANOEL FERNANDES PRETEL
AMALIA JIMENES GARCIA

Examples of work, dignity and faithfulness

"Que sea lo que Diós quiera."

To Lucimar, my beloved wife, friend and companion, who
for more than forty years has been my partner
in ministry and has helped me to be faithful
to our Lord Jesus Christ.
To our sons, Victor Manoel, Daniel Conrado and Marcos
Raphael, who have made us happy on our journey.

"Make me to know your ways, O Lord*;*
teach me your paths.
Lead me in your truth, and teach me"
– Psalm 25:4-5a

Acknowledgements

Deo gratias.

1 Corinthians 15:57, 2 Corinthians 2:14

Looking back, I am very grateful to God for what He has done in my life. Before I was born, my mother dedicated me to the Lord and He accepted her offering. I always had an inclination toward the spiritual things of life. I accepted Jesus and was baptized when I was still a child. Pastor João Gomes taught me the plan of God for my life, and since then I have never been alone. He was always with me, on good days and bad days, in happiness or sadness. In everything, I have felt His guiding hands on me.

I would like to remember and give thanks for several servants of Jesus Christ, who have counselled and helped me in the beginning and throughout my studies for the ministry – my dear uncle Rev. Antonio Jimenes Garcia, who was the first person with whom I shared my call; my cousin Rev. Antonio Villar Garcia, with whom, many times, I talked about the challenges of pastoral service; Rev. Werner Kaschell, who graciously received me in his office at the Colégio Batista Brasileiro in São Paulo and offered me tuition and a place to live and work at the school; Rev. Dr. Thurmon Bryant, Southern Baptist missionary, Principal of the São Paulo Faculdade Teológica Batista (Baptist Seminary), with whom I worked as Secretary; Rev. Alberto Blanco de Oliveira, whose Berean Mission helped churches in need in the State of Amazonas; and Rev. Eneas Tognini, a man of prayer. I will never forget that day, in his office, when he invited me to kneel and pray with him for those who did not understand his involvement in the Spiritual Renewal Movement. It has been a precious lesson that has helped me in difficult situations in the ministry when things were challenging.

My special gratitude goes also to Rev. David Doonan, a missionary with the Baptist Missionary Society of London, England, (BMS) whom I met working in his mission field in Umuarama, in the State of Paraná, Brazil. He suggested my name to the Principal of Spurgeon's College, Dr. G. R. Beasley-Murray. At this most prestigious institution of theological studies, I was a student for three years. My thanks go as well to Rev. and Mrs. John Clifford Parsons, ex-missionaries in Angola, Africa, with the Baptist Missionary Society, who became our "adopted parents" during our days in London, England. With all of them I learned that the ministry requires love, patience, persistence and constant prayer. God is faithful and we are only ambassadors of His kingdom.

I would like also to give thanks to Mr. and Mrs. Roy Taylor, who, since we arrived in Canada, have been like adopted grandparents for our children. They have given so much of their time helping immigrants who have made of this great country their new home. Ever since I came to know Rev. Jack Anderson, Pastor at Central Baptist Church, Oakville, Ontario, he was a wonderful friend who always helped me to be faithful in the ministry. As he always said, "God called us to be faithful and not successful."

My gratitude goes to all who have encouraged me to write my memoirs – family, friends, my wonderful sons and my beloved wife for editing the manuscript in the Portuguese language. I would also like to thank my cousin Rev. Haroldo Rico, pastor of Igreja Batista Centenário (Centennial Baptist Church) in São Paulo, Brazil, who kindly did a review of the Portuguese language edition. I am very grateful to Warren McBurney and Mary Coggins for their gracious help in editing the English edition, improving it greatly. To God be all honour and praise for what He is and does for all who trust in Him. He showed me His ways, taught me His path and led me in His truth (Psalm 25:.4-5a).

This is a book of memories. I tell stories that happened throughout the years of my life – my background, call, preparation and ministry. I show how God, since the time I was born, was leading my walk in such a way that I knew I was not alone. He was always with me and helped me at every step, in order to carry out the pastoral and missionary ministry. In fellowship with the Lord Jesus Christ I learned the secret of being content in every circumstance (Philippians 4:12b GNT).

Rev. João Fernandes Garcia
Oakville, Ontario, Canada
December 2017

Contents

BACKGROUND

1. SPANISH IMMIGRATION 3
2. I'LL BE BACK NEXT SUNDAY 9
3. MY CASHEW TREE 15
4. POPCORN CART 21
5. BIG BEE 29
6. DIFFERENT WAYS 37

CALL AND PREPARATION

7. THE GOOD SAMARITAN 47
8. REVOLUTION 61
9. A SPACIOUS BASEMENT APARTMENT 67
10. CAN I HELP? 73
11. ABBEY ROAD, LONDON, ENGLAND, 1969 77
12. SPURGEON'S COLLEGE 93
13. LOVE LETTERS FROM HERE AND THERE 97
14. ON THE BANKS OF THE LIS RIVER, LEIRIA, PORTUGAL 105
15. MEMORIES OF LONDON, ENGLAND 113
16. THE SS *PASTEUR* 119

MNISTRY

17. THE LAND OF THE ARAUCARIA TREES 129
18. PRINCESS OF THE FIELDS 135
19. ON THE BANKS OF THE OTHER THAMES RIVER 139
20. FROM SADNESS TO JOY (From Baca to Beracah) 155

21. ON THE SHORE OF LAKE ONTARIO 163
22. SOWING THE WORD.. 175
23. MISSION IN THE AZORES 185
24. MISSION IN CUBA: Christianity Is Not an Idea........................... 189

APPENDIX
25. HERITAGE FROM THE LORD 197
26. JETE, GRANADA, SPAIN 204

BACKGROUND

1

&

SPANISH IMMIGRATION

"The journey, not the destination, matters…"
– *T. S. Eliot*

Between 1880 and 1960, about seven hundred and fifty thousand Spaniards from the Provinces of Galicia and Andalucía, emigrated to South America.[1] Among them were my paternal grandparents **Rafael Fernandes Peres and Dolores Armendro Pretel** and my maternal grandparents **Antonio Garcia Castilho and Carmen Jimenes Garcia.** Rafael (40 years old) and Dolores (38 years old) left the village of Jete, Suspiro del Moro, south of Granada, in the Province of Andalucía, Spain, taking with them their children Josefa (14 years old),[2] Francisco (8 years old), Manoel (5 years old) and Gabriel (1 year old). On August 28, 1904, they left Málaga, Spain, on the steamship *Espagne*, in third class, together with many other Spaniards, on a long journey down south on the Atlantic Ocean. The *Espagne* arrived in the port of Santos, São Paulo, Brazil, on

---

[1] *Wikipedia*, under the words "Spanish immigration to Brazil."
[2] She died before arriving in Brazil.

September 17 of the same year. Antonio (38 years old) and Carmen (37 years old) of Albuñuelas, south of Granada, in the Province of Andalucía, Spain, left from the port of Málaga, Spain, on the steamship *Espagne* on October 8, 1908, arriving at the port of Santos, São Paulo, on November 1 of the same year. They took with them their children Amparo (14 years old), Asencion (13 years old), Amalia (8 years old), Antonio (6 years old), Maria (3 years old) and Carmen (1 year old).[3]

They all arrived with great expectations for a better life, for, in Spain in those days, there was not very much work and they were having great financial difficulties in living. Emigrating to Brazil was a wonderful opportunity to start a new life. Brazil, with so many coffee plantation farms, was in need of people to work. It was known as a land of milk and honey. I acquired this information in May 2011 when I visited the small city of Jete, where my father had been born. On that occasion I asked the mayor of Jete why so many Spaniards emigrated to Brazil in the early 1900s. His answer was, "*Hambre. No habia trabajo; teniam que emigrar.*" (Hunger. There was no work; they had to emigrate.)

At the beginning of last century, in Brazil, the coffee plantation farms, especially in the State of São Paulo, needed workers. The slaves had been recently freed, on May 13, 1888, through a law signed by Princess Isabel.[4] Free, they ran away from the coffee plantations. The farm owners did not have any other alternative but to look for a cheap work force in Europe. They found in the Spaniards good workers who could replace the slaves. With the help of the Brazilian government, the coffee farm owners brought thousands of workers, especially to the State of São Paulo.

My paternal grandparents, Rafael and Dolores, intended to stay in Brazil for only five years and then go back to Spain, perhaps rich! They took with them to Brazil their three sons Francisco, Manoel and Gabriel and their daughter Josefa. The boys grew up on the coffee

---

[3] Two other children, Manuel and Helena, were born in Brazil.
[4] Princess Isabel was the eldest daughter of Pedro II, Emperor of Brazil. She was born in Rio de Janeiro on July 29, 1846, and died in France November 14, 1921. She was Imperial Princess of Brazil from January 9, 1850, to December 5, 1891. She signed the law that gave freedom to the slaves in Brazil on May 13, 1888.

plantation, but, unfortunately, the girl Josefa died on the long and exhausting trip from Málaga to Santos.[5] She was buried at sea. The sadness of my grandparents must have been intense. My maternal grandparents also brought with them their children, five daughters, Amparo, Asencion, Amalia, Maria and Carmen, and a son, Antonio. It was a long and difficult trip, with little food and medicine, travelling in third class on a steamship.

The other Spanish families also saw their children grow up on the coffee plantation farms around the city of Jaú, in the State of São Paulo. Unfortunately, I did not have the privilege of knowing my grandparents. I vaguely remember seeing my maternal grandmother only once, when I went to visit my married sister Carmen in São Paulo in January 1958.

After a long trip south crossing the Atlantic, in approximately twenty-one days, the steamship *Espagne* arrived at the port of Santos, São Paulo. According to the information in the Public Archives of the State of São Paulo,[6] all immigrants were registered on their arrival and taken by train to the immigrants hostel at Bras, São Paulo.[7] They were welcomed, treated and fed. Interviewed by the farmers that hired them, they were taken by train to the coffee plantations.

Many Spaniards, including my grandparents and their children, were hired by farmers around the city of Jaú, in the State of São Paulo. When I was a little boy, many times after dinner, in the conversations around the wood stove, I heard the expression in the Spanish language that is still in my mind *"en la rueda de Jahu,"* which meant "in the environs of the city of Jaú." They were great workers, but, unfortunately, they were poorly paid. The fortune that they waited for never came. They lived all their lives in Brazil, without ever going back to Spain, not even for a short visit. They were deceived with the promise that they would become rich working on the coffee plantations in the State of São Paulo, planting and harvesting the coffee that was known as *"the green gold."* However, they worked for housing, food, medicines and clothes. At the end of each month they did not have any money left. The children did not

---

[5] The Museum of Immigration in São Paulo
[6] See my document file, "Familia Garcia," on *Facebook*.
[7] Immigrants Hostel, Bras, Visconde de Parnaiba, 1316, São Paulo

learn to read or write because there were no schools on the coffee plantation.

It was the general thinking in those days that there was no need for the workers to learn reading, writing, mathematics or history. Therefore, the immigrants did not have to go to school! They lived practically like the slaves that had just received their freedom. My parents, Manoel Fernandes Pretel[8] and Amalia Jimenes Garcia, grew up on the same coffee plantation "in the environs of the city of Jaú." They met, fell in love, and were married in the city of Jaú on December 19, 1924. Their first residence was on the same coffee plantation farm where many other Spaniards lived. The first children soon came – Moises, Rafael and Dolores. They died as children, attacked by childhood diseases.

The climate in the vicinity was not very good for my mother. When she was stricken by a fearsome disease, the medical doctor encouraged my parents to move to another region where the climate would be more favourable for my mother. With all their possessions on a cart, they moved to another coffee plantation called Goataporanga, not far from the city of Herculândia in the West of the State of São Paulo. There my mother was healed. Then they could work so that the children could grow up healthy. My mother could never explain why their first three children died. In those days, there was no vaccination for childhood diseases. When she spoke about it, tears came from her eyes, remembering those difficult and sad days. Moises, the first child, was nine years old when he died, and the other two still younger. The other children who were born afterward were all healthy – Antonio, Carmen, Samuel, Daniel, Paulo, Rute, João, Emilia (Miriam) and Sarah.

With the passing years, their children married and had their own children:

Antonio married Creusa, and they had eight children: Valdeci, Wilson, Marcos, Vera, Sônia, Paulo, Jorge and Sérgio.

Carmen married Euclides; they did not have children.

---

[8] Pretel is not a very common name, but in the district of Granada, Spain, there are many families with this surname. The origin of this name could be from India, a modification of Patel, or from France.

Samuel married Teresinha, and they had four children: Shirley, Silas, Elizeu and Eliane.

Daniel married Luiza, and they had five children: Ezequiel, Elizete, Débora, Paulo and Regina. He divorced Luiza and lived with Fatima, and they had two children: Lucas Daniel and Pedro André.

Paulo married Enóe, and they had two children: Ana and Valéria.

Rute married Samuel, and they had one child and adopted another: Rubens and Kelly (adopted).

João married Lucimar in London, England, and they had three children: Victor Manoel and Daniel Conrado in Brazil and Marcos Raphael in Canada.

Emilia (Miriam) married Paulo; they did not have children.

Sarah married Cláudio, and they had two children: Priscíla and Patrícia.

Life was not very easy for my parents on the coffee plantation. They worked very hard and also took care of their large family. They were religious people and followed the traditions of the Catholic Church. They were devotees, but without the knowledge of salvation that only Jesus Christ offers to those who believe in Him. They heard the gospel for the first time from a missionary lady who had just arrived from Latvia, one of the Balkan countries, and who lived on the community farm of Palma, near where my parents lived.

2

&

I'LL BE BACK NEXT SUNDAY

*"Commit your way to the LORD;
trust in him, and he will act."
– Psalm 37:5*

One day, a lady came to our home, at the Goataporanga coffee farm, not too far from the city of Herculândia, in the State of São Paulo. Senhora Maria Melemberg was a missionary known as *Dona Maria Leta* (Miss Maria Latvian) to the Spanish immigrants who lived on the coffee farms. She always carried a Bible with her. She was invited to come in and explain to my mother, who was very curious, what she was really teaching.

Senhora Maria Melemberg walked fifteen kilometres to reach that farm where my parents lived. She came from a colony where there lived about two thousand people who had immigrated to Brazil from Latvia, a Baltic country that was taken over by the Russian Marxist Revolution of 1917. They were running away from the religious persecution that transformed their country into a communist country, closing churches and forbidding their members to meet.

In those days of persecution, the Latvian Baptists prayed to God and received a vision of a distant country in South America where they could live in freedom and peace and practise their faith freely. They bought inexpensive land from the government of the State of São Paulo, in the region of Alta Paulista. They founded the colony of Palma, a community of immigrant people from Latvia. They cleared the forest, worked the land and built houses, a place of worship and a school.

Among them, there were several Baptist pastors and a special sister with the gift of evangelism. Sent by the Baptist church of Palma, she would visit the surrounding farms preaching the gospel, carrying the Bible with her. By this time other relatives of my parents were also living on the same farm of Goataporanga. Every Sunday they would gather in one of the houses to listen to the missionary talking about Jesus Christ – my parents, their children, uncles, aunties, cousins and other Spanish friends. They were very attentive and listened very carefully. They understood the message and accepted Jesus as their Saviour. At the end of each meeting the missionary lady always said, "I'll be back next Sunday" – a promise made and kept! The people would wait anxiously for her, to listen and to learn more about the gospel.

In the picture on the following page, the reader can see a group of converted Spaniards. They were baptized in the Rio Feio (Ugly River), not too far from Herculândia, on whose banks the community of Palma was founded. My mother and other ladies gathered all their ornaments, jewels and idols, put everything in a bag, walked to the river and, before being baptized, threw the bag into the river. The current took away what was an impediment for them to follow Jesus Christ. From that moment on they were different persons and should live as such.

Dr. Vivian M. Gruber, a professor at Wayland University, Plainview, Texas, wrote a doctoral thesis about the movement of the Latvian immigrants to Brazil. The thesis was published in a magazine called *Humanities and Science*. She wrote, "The Latvians who immigrated to Brazil impelled by religion were, for the most part, Baptists." She described in this thesis how these Latvian Baptists founded churches, set up weekend schools to teach children to read and write, began a program of basic health care and sanitation education and, above all, taught the Bible and choral music, so much a part of the Baltic peoples, and evangelized the Brazilian families that lived around the community of Varpa and Palma, but also the European people, especially the Spaniards who lived in the same region, many of whom had taken the place of the slaves on the coffee farms.[9]

A group of Spanish Baptist Christians, immigrants to Brazil

One sunny morning, before going to the coffee harvest, my father said to my mother in Spanish, *"Vamos a la ciudad para que los niños estudien en la escuela."* ("Let's move to the city so that our children can go to school.") She totally agreed, for this had been her prayer since the moment she learned how to pray. It did not take too long to pack up the little furniture they had and, with their children on the top of a horse cart, they left the coffee plantation farm and moved into a small rented house in a poor area of the nearby city of Herculândia.

---

[9] Wayland Baptist University, Plainview, Texas, USA, "The Balts in Brazil: A Northern Minority in a Southern Country" by Dr. Vivian M. Gruber

My father had great difficulty finding a job, since he had always worked in a coffee plantation and never had any experience working in another job. The conversation with my mother, always in Spanish, started with a question. *"Ahora que voy hacer?"* ("Now what am I going to do?")

Those conversations around the wood stove, after dinner, resulted in a great idea – what about going to the farmers around the town, buying vegetables and watermelons and reselling them door to door? In those days, people in a small town like Herculândia bought their vegetables at the door. The sellers would come with their horse cart and sell the vegetables for a reasonable price. My father decided he was able to do that. He had a horse and a cart that he had brought from the farm; therefore, he could start his own business. He used to bring the cart full of vegetables and watermelons. Sometimes I helped him to bring them inside the house for storage. Then, when everything was inside, my father would get a large watermelon, he cut it in several slices and we all ate the fresh, red, delicious watermelon. Life was simple, but there was plenty of food that made us all very happy.

We attended the local Baptist church. It was a very pretty white building, with an impressive tower. The entrance had several steps leading up to the front door. At this time my uncle Antonio Garcia, my mother's brother, was studying for the ministry at the Bible school in Palma and was the student pastor of that church. Later on, he finished his studies, was ordained to the ministry and became the senior pastor. He lived with his family beside the church. Years later, he and his family moved to the city of São Paulo, where he planted a church in the subdivision of Vila Formosa, at 95 Saigon Street.

Many years later, before I moved to London, Ontario, Canada, with my family, to be a missionary among Portuguese people, I visited that Baptist church in Herculândia. I wanted to do some research in the church books on the business meetings of those days. Unfortunately, I never found them, in either the church or any other place. Maybe they never existed!

All nine of us, plus my parents, living in a small house was not easy. As the older brothers were old enough to work and in need of learning a trade, we moved to a bigger city called Tupã, not too far from Herculândia. *"Vamonos a otra ciudad onde halla mas condiciones para que los hijos aprendam una profission,*" my father would say to my mother.

In Tupã,[10] my father bought a buggy and a very nice horse. He worked carrying passengers who arrived at the train station from different places to their houses or hotels. He was stationed at the train depot. It was in this activity that he met a man of Japanese descent who was a tailor and had his own business in Tupã. His name was Jorge, to this day well known in the family. In those days, everyone went to the a*lfaiataria* (tailoring) shop to have their suits made. The great department stores did not exist in those days, and suits were made by hand and by machines with pedals. So, it was an excellent trade for us to learn. My father then asked Mr. Jorge whether he could teach the trade to my older brother Antonio. So, he learned and taught my other two brothers Samuel and Daniel. I was taught a few years later when we lived in another city called Mandaguaçu. My brothers worked for years in this trade, and opened their own business.

---

[10] Tupã is a municipality in the State of São Paulo, Brazil. It is located in the Alta Paulista region, 530 kilometres from the city of São Paulo. Tupã means "Thunder" in the Tupi language.

3

&

MY CASHEW TREE

"What you sow does not come to life unless it dies."
– Paul the Apostle in 1 Corinthians 15:36b

In the forties, the first cars began arriving in Tupã, an important city in the State of São Paulo, surrounded by coffee plantation farms. Fords and Chevrolets were, of course, faster than the "horse and carriage" way of transportation those days. The carriage pulled by the strength of an animal needed extra care in the face of new challenges. My father had a beautiful horse. He took very good care of it. Sometimes he would travel outside the city to buy a special grass to feed the animal. He cut the hay, and I helped, making mounds of it. One day, somewhat careless, my father cut his finger with the scythe and the blood was pouring out. It was then that I learned an interesting and useful lesson, about what urine can be used for! He went to a corner and urinated in the cut and immediately the blood flow came to a halt. Urine is a powerful antibiotic. It is a perfect medicine for our bodies and it is always available.[11] We headed home with the hay, and the slender horse was ready for its meal.

A few days afterwards, my dad, returning home from a long day's work, had a serious accident. A *Pé de Bode* (Goat), a nickname for a 1940 Ford car, travelling at a high speed, crashed into the buggy, destroying it and the horse, who had to be put down right at the scene.

In the evening, our house was full of people, friends who came to visit us. Fortunately, nothing had happened to my father, but the concern was where my father would find another job. *"Que voy hacer?"* ("Where am I to work?") He had no insurance and no money to buy another buggy and horse. Those were very difficult days! We were Christians, of course, and prayed that God would provide any kind of job for my father. And God always has the best for those who trust in Him. We are never alone! We were led by Him, as Paul wrote to the church in Rome, "We know that all things work together for good for those who love God, who are called according to his purpose" (Romans 8:28).

Lavínia is a small city in the West of the State of São Paulo, reached by train on the Estrada de Ferro Noroeste (Northwest Railway Line). It was growing very quickly with investments in the coffee plantations. A sister of my mother, Amparo, married a man who was the administrator of a large coffee farm. With his savings, he bought his own small farm in the outskirts of Lavínia. My uncle Emílio was looking for a good and trustworthy family to rent it on the basis of half and half profit sharing, for he had no time to work on his own small farm. It was providential that my father was available. When he received the news that "Uncle Manoel" was looking for a job, he immediately went to meet him in Tupã, not too far from Lavínia. They talked about the details of the work that had to be done on the farm and my father accepted the terms. Soon he started preparations to move to Lavínia.

It didn't take too long to fill a truck with all we had and load the children, eight of us,[12] on the back, headed away to the unknown

---

[11] Christy, Martha. Urine: Your Own Perfect Medicine. *All-Natural Natural Healing Resource Centre*. Retrieved 2019 from all-natural.com/natural-remedies/urine/

[12] Antonio, Carmen, Samuel, Daniel, Paulo, Rute, João and Miriam. Sarah had not been born yet.

city of Lavínia. We left Tupã at night and travelled all night, along dusty and bumpy roads. The next morning, we arrived at our destination, a small farm where there was a nice house, recently built for our family. We were all very happy, in spite of a long journey on the back of a truck! There, in that small city, my parents had the opportunity to start all over again.

I was born at the Goataporanga farm, in the outskirts of Herculândia, in the State of São Paulo, on March 26, 1942. However, I was registered on May 10, 1942. I have no idea why I was registered later! Probably because they lived on a farm, on a coffee plantation, and my father had to wait until he had several things to do in the city and was allowed to go downtown, where the registry office was located.

When I was seven years old, I was enrolled in the public school, Grupo Escolar Joaquim Franco de Melo, in Lavínia, which was located beyond a beautiful park and the railway station. There I had my first school teacher, who lived in another city and came by train to teach. I walked every day from the small farm where we lived to the school, together with my brother Daniel, also a student. I was so happy to be able to go to school and learn to read and write. But it was at that school that I suffered bullying. One day, going home after studies, I was walking with a group of children. Among them there was one who was always bothering and trying to attack me. I did not have any other alternative but to run fast, until I reached the first tree in the avenue, and I climbed it very quickly. Apparently, he did not see me in the top of the tree or he gave up running as fast as I was.

That area of the city of Lavínia is separated from the downtown by a bridge that was built over the railway, close to the train station. To go to school, we had to walk over this bridge every day. I enjoyed seeing the trains arriving from São Paulo, and those that were stationed on the railroad tracks. So many of them! All of them bringing food from the big cities and carrying back sacks and sacks of good coffee and cotton produced at the various farms around Lavínia.

At the small farm where we lived, my parents had many chickens. My job was to collect the eggs that they produced every day and sell them in the restaurant of the train that came from São Paulo. The money was given as an offering for missions at the local Baptist church, to which we belonged. It was at this small train station that my brother Paulo started learning Morse code, which helped him become a transmitter of text information for the Brazilian Army, where he worked for many years until his retirement as a major.

Rev. João Gomes travelled once a month from Muritinga do Sul, in the State of São Paulo, where he was the senior pastor. He was the visiting pastor at our church in Lavínia. He always stayed in our home at the small farm, every weekend that he came.

"João, today is the day to pick up the pastor at the train station; come, let's go," my father would call to me.

I liked to go with him. When the pastor arrived, I asked him to let me carry his suitcase. We walked to the small farm and he stayed with us for that weekend. It was a joy to have him at our home. We talked a lot! One sunny Sunday morning, before breakfast, he was outside our house, sitting on a chair and quietly reading a book. I approached him and asked what he was reading. "What are you reading?"

"I am reading the Bible," he answered.

That morning Pastor João Gomes taught me the plan of salvation. He read John 3:16 and Psalm 23, and explained to me in detail what I had to do to have Jesus as my Saviour. When I showed an interest, he prayed with me. One Sunday, at an evening service, I responded, coming to the altar together with other people. Then I was enrolled in the special orientation class for baptism. One Sunday afternoon, I was baptized in the water of a small river around the city of Lavínia. After the baptism, all those who were baptized plus the congregation walked together back to the city and our houses, singing hymns and praising God. We were all very happy, full of joy and greatly excited to be part of a wonderful group of people who follow Jesus. I was only seven years old and since that moment I have never stopped following Jesus Christ. He has always been with me and has guided my ways. I could not see the kind of future that God had for me. I was only a child, but God had already beforehand traced a path on which I would walk. He had set me apart (Romans 8:29-30), and He was leading me. I was not alone, never alone.

The Casa Moreira, a well-known supply store, bought the potatoes produced on our farm every year. I remember the day my father came back with a full truckload of sacks of potatoes that he had taken to be sold. That day Casa Moreira did not buy the potatoes because they were not as good as the year before. My father was very sad! The potatoes had to be sold for a low price to another buyer. It was a great loss but, being Christians, we took it to the Lord in prayer. The whole family met together and prayed that God would comfort us and provide a new place where my father could sell the potatoes. It did not take too long for someone to come and buy that year's whole crop.

On our small farm, we had everything – potatoes, onions, garlic, cotton, an orchard and some dairy cows. One day I planted a cashew nut, which I saw grow and produce fruit. I made a small hole, planted a cashew nut there and waited until it would spring out of the ground. One morning after drinking my coffee and milk, and eating a slice of bread, I ran to the place where I had planted the cashew. It was a great joy for a boy like me to see that it had sprung from the soil. With the passing days, I saw it grow, become a beautiful tree and produce fruit. It was exciting to live on a small farm where we had so many plants all producing fruits.

After so many years I still remember my cashew tree that taught me the great lesson that the Apostle Paul wrote to the church of Corinth (I Corinthians 15), about the resurrection of Jesus. When we sow a seed, it needs to die in order to grow. We plant a small seed and it dies, springs up, grows and produces fruit. This is a metaphor of our Christian life, following Jesus who leads us on our journey. We have died in Christ and in baptism we were buried with Him and resurrected in order to live a new life.

It was a fascinating time to live in Lavínia. One day, however, my uncle Rev. Antonio Garcia, who was the pastor of Vila Formosa Baptist Church, in the city of São Paulo, came to visit us. He brought with him his daughter Letícia and her friend Tilza. They both became close friends with my sister Carmen. My uncle, a wonderful servant of Jesus, had a long conversation with my parents about what was happening in the big city of São Paulo, after World War II. Industry was growing quickly, and it would be a great opportunity for my parents to start all over again in a big city like São Paulo.

4

&

POPCORN CART

*"You are never too old to set another goal
or to dream a new dream."*
– C. S. Lewis

After the Second World War, in the fifties, there was a fantastic growth of industry in Brazil.[13] The factories in São Paulo were hiring labourers from different parts of Brazil. My parents liked the idea of starting again and now in a big city. So, they allowed my sister Carmen to go with my uncle Rev. Antonio Garcia, pastor of Vila Formosa Baptist Church, São Paulo, his daughter Letícia and a friend named Tilza. We all would go later, when everything was organized. When Uncle Emílio, the owner of the small farm in Lavínia where my father was the administrator, knew that my parents were thinking of moving to São Paulo, he was not very happy. He tried to convince

---

[13] "The Brazilian Industry in the fifties," analysis written by Ana Claudia Caputo and Hildete Pereira de Melo (Google)

them not to go. However, the decision had already been made; we would move very soon.

By this time my eldest brother, Antonio, had already left home; he wanted to have his independence. He moved to a city called Oswaldo Cruz, a new and prosperous city in the State of São Paulo. There he found work as a tailor. He lived in a hotel. In that city, he met a young girl called Creusa Fernandes. Later they married and moved to Maringá, in the State of Paraná, but didn't stay there very long. They moved again to a small pioneer town, not too far from Maringá, called "*Cala a Boca*" ("Shut Up"), as it was known in those days, the town of Mandaguaçu, in the State of Paraná. There he started his own business, a tailoring shop, that he gave the name of *Alfaiataria Garcia* (Garcia's Tailoring). They lived at the rear of his business building, in a small rented apartment. It was there that his first son, Valdeci, was born.

For many years the coffee production was excellent. In any city or town, we could see sacks and sacks of coffee stored in large warehouses. The buyers would go to the coffee farms and negotiate the price with the owners, then buy and transport it to the warehouses. The movement of carts and trucks carrying coffee was huge. Then they waited until the price went up to sell, so that they would make a better profit.

Because of the great amount of coffee produced, the Brazilian government had already approved a law in 1931 to burn the excess coffee production.[14] This law was applied in the State of Paraná in the fifties.

If my parents, instead of moving to São Paulo, had gone to the North in the State of Paraná, they would have had better financial conditions. They could have bought cheap land good for coffee plantation, the best agricultural product at that moment. To this day when our family meets for a special event we always talk about this lost opportunity. But this was only a speculation, nothing else. The fact was that they moved to the big city of São Paulo.

One day in 1949, about noon, we took a train of the Estrada de Ferro Noroeste (Northwest Railway Line), at Lavínia, which took us

---

[14] Law about the burning of coffee during the Getúlio Vargas government, in 1931

to the big city of São Paulo. We were nine of us – my father, mother, Samuel, Daniel, Paulo, Rute, João, Miriam and Sarah. Titio, my dark-coloured dog, stayed behind. I was very sad and he was too. We all liked him a lot. At that moment, when we all were departing, I remembered what had happened to him one night.

We were all sleeping, all was quiet on the farm, and we could see through cracks in the wooden walls and doors of our house that the moon was shining. It was a beautiful summer night. Suddenly we heard a noise, "Pufff!", followed by a barking dog. My father woke up, turned on the lamp and ran outside, to check on what was happening. We all followed him. The barking was from Titio, coming from down inside the water well. Every night he jumped onto the cover of the well to sleep there. That night someone had left the well uncovered and when Titio jumped he went down thirty-two metres! There was a great noise that was heard from afar. He was down there in the water trying to swim and crying at the same time. It was then that all of us said at the same time, "Calm down Titio, we are going to save you!" And we repeated once again, "Don't cry, we are going to save you."

But he was barking, and barking without stopping, as if trying to say, "Help, help, I am drowning!" He knew our voices.

My father let down a bucket tied to a rope. We all shouted out together, "Titio, get into the bucket!" as if he understood the Portuguese language. And probably he did! It didn't take too many tries for him to get into it. Very carefully my father pulled him up, and he was saved. What a very happy moment for him that dawn. We took him into the house. The rest of that night he slept with us, in our room. In a tropical country, the dog's house is outside. He must have been very frightened, going down in a water well. Dogs have feelings too! Moving to São Paulo, we left him behind in Lavínia. We never knew what happened to him.

The train to São Paulo always passed close to the entrance of our small farm and that of the warehouse of Sanbra cotton; we could see for the last time, through the train's window, the place where we had spent a wonderful time for a few years. It had been a life of hard work, but there my parents earned sufficient money and saved what was needed for our days in São Paulo.

Later that afternoon the train stopped at Araçatuba station. About midnight we arrived in Bauru, where we had to change trains.

We took all our baggage and boarded a train that was coming from Marília, and going to São Paulo. We arrived at the Estação da Luz (Light Station) in the morning. São Paulo! I never thought I would one day live in such a big city – the beautiful Jardim da Luz (Light Garden), so many cars that I had never seen before, trams and buses going east and west, north and south, a lot of people walking quickly, rushing for work! Carmen, my sister, was waiting for us. We took taxis that carried us and our baggage, through very busy traffic, to Vila Formosa, to the house of my uncle and aunt Rev. and Mrs. Antonio Garcia, who received us with open arms, ready to help as much as they could. They were very good to us. I never forgot what they did for our family. It is impossible to imagine one home receiving another nine people. Our wonderful uncle, aunt and cousins accepted us!

Early the next day was the beginning of a drama, some unexpected circumstances that happened to our family. It was impossible to find a large house for rent. We were a big family! Where to find a house that would accommodate all of us? And we needed one that would not cost too much. Our new beginning in São Paulo was disappointing and sad.

We continued living with our uncle and aunt for a few days. Finally, my father found a house to rent on 73rd Street in Vila Formosa. However, it was a house built above the street level. We had to walk up some steps to get to the door. It was a large house that accommodated all of us, and we moved into it, a good and clean home.

The next step was for my father to look for a job. There was a real need for workers in those days. It was natural that he would find one quite easily. My brothers Samuel and Daniel, because they were tailors, found work immediately at a tailoring shop in Água Rasa. Carmen was already working at a pharmaceutical company called Laboratório Morifarma. The worst thing that happened to us was not finding a job for my father. He was 51 years of age! It was very difficult! Many times, my mother would stay for a long time kneeling and praying, behind a door of one of the rooms. She was a very faithful woman.

It was then that my father had a good idea, from what he might have seen as he walked around on the streets of Vila Formosa. He was a very good worker and never had been without a job. He could not be waiting for money to come from heaven! Those days, mobile amusement rides came regularly to Vila Formosa and were stationed at the main square, where 73rd Street began. He had a great idea, thought about it and put it into practice. He went to a carpentry shop and asked the carpenter to make him a cart, with rubber wheels, to be used to sell popcorn in front of the amusement rides. Every night he would fill the cart with popcorn, sweets and peanuts and would go to sell them in front of the amusement rides. I always accompanied him. I was his helper! The cart was heavy. He was always tired, and still had to push it back to the house, some steps above the street level. He always needed help. With a rope, one of my brothers would pull the cart up while my father would push it until it reached the front of the house. I liked to be with him; it was a small help, but when we arrived home, always later in the night, it was very sad to see him so tired. Nevertheless, that was our life in those days.

Every day, after the night work at the amusement rides there were leftovers. My mother had a bright idea, as she did not want them put into the garbage. She would make small packages with popcorn and sweets and asked me to sell them door to door next morning. As I was not registered for school yet, I walked all morning and I managed to sell almost everything my mother had prepared. Most of the days I came back home with my basket empty. Sometimes I did not sell everything but would not miss, in any case, passing by the variety store and buying my favourite coconut candy. Savouring this delicious candy, I would join the other children to play a soccer match on 73rd Street before returning home.

My mother tried to register me at the public school of Vila Formosa. We lined up for a long time, but when our turn came the secretary told us to return another day. So, I was not registered. Many families had come to São Paulo looking for a better life; therefore, there were too many children to go to school, not enough space and too few teachers. I went back home very sad and quiet, because I wanted to continue studying in my second year at public school. Ever since I was a child, I wanted to study; that was always my desire. God was guiding my paths, even though that school had closed its doors to me.

Jacob, my cousin, became my great friend. We were still children, but we used to walk for hours on the streets of Vila Formosa. Sometimes, Sunday afternoons, we would go to watch a soccer match in a restaurant, on Eduardo Cotching Avenue, that had one of the first television sets in that area of São Paulo. Bandeirantes TV broadcast the final match of the Paulista Championship of Soccer. For the first time, I was watching TV. I was amazed! It was very difficult to understand that a box could show my beloved Corinthians playing against Portuguesa Desportos! Corinthians won and were the champions for the thirteenth time in 1951. Portuguesa came in third place.

We did not stay too long in São Paulo, and life was very difficult. After about one year the money my father had saved in Lavínia was running out. Life was getting worse and worse! Happiness had given place to sadness. None of us were happy in São Paulo. We were praying that God would show us a place that would be better for us. When my mother began to sing a hymn that she liked very much, I knew that some difficulties were going on. Many times, her beautiful voice, with a mixture of Spanish and Portuguese, spread through the house. "Christ loved me and freed me; His immense love changed me" (Hymn 46, *Cantor Christão*).

It was a sad day at home; after we prayed, I went out with my basket full of popcorn and sweets, leftovers from the night before, to sell them on the street. But I sold only a little; that day I was not in the mood for walking and knocking door to door. I preferred to play soccer with my friends.

Suddenly, a taxi drove close to where we were playing. The soccer ball stopped rolling. All the children stared at the taxi. A young man got out and recognized me. He called my name, "João!"

I did not know who he was, and why he was calling me.

He continued, saying, "I am Antonio, your brother."

I would not have recognized him if he hadn't said who he was.

"Where are you living? I have been looking for where you live for a long time. I was going back to Paraná because I couldn't find your house."

I was so happy when he said he was my brother. He had left home when my parents decided to move to São Paulo. He was now living in the North of the State of Paraná.[15] I left my friends and the

---

[15] A land development company owned by Lord Lovat from England, with a group of investors, had bought a large area of land and was developing it, selling it in

soccer ball, took my basket, got into the car and directed the driver to my house. That day I forgot to buy my delicious coconut candy! I was very happy my brother met me. It seems incredible, but in the previous few days my parents had been talking about him, how he was and where he lived, and then he just arrived. What a surprise!

We arrived at home and walked up the stairs that took us to the door of the house. My mother, when she saw us, shouted, "Antonio, my son!"

My father, who was taking care of some chickens we had in the backyard, ran into the house. We all embraced and cried. We were a united, sentimental family.

Dinner that day was very festive! Antonio was informed of what was really happening with us in São Paulo. Things were not going well. My father could not find a job. Expenses were high; there was not enough money to cover them.

"You must go to live in the North of Paraná," Antonio said, and then he continued, "I am living in a new town not too far from Maringá. I opened my own business. Samuel and Daniel could work for me. Father could open a grocery store, which is needed in the town." How encouraging for all of us!

Only Carmen, our darling "Tatá," did not agree to move. She decided to stay in São Paulo living with our uncle and aunt Rev. and Mrs. Antonio Garcia. She was working at a good pharmaceutical company, Laboratório Morifarma, and did not want to leave it. The popcorn cart stayed leaning on the wall of the 73rd Street house; the basket was forgotten somewhere in the house; I did not have any use for it anymore. We left São Paulo for Mandaguaçu, in the State of Paraná. Another unforgettable chapter of my life was about to begin.

---

small lots. As the land was good for coffee, people from São Paulo and other states of Brazil and Europe purchased land and planted coffee.

5

BIG BEE

"Pay attention to your teacher and learn all you can."
– Proverbs 23:12 (GNT)

It was with deep sadness that I had to say goodbye to my great friend and cousin Jacob, with whom I had walked many times around Vila Formosa. We were part of the children's group of the local Baptist church in that subdivision of the city of São Paulo. I also gave a great hug to my uncle Rev. Antonio Garcia and aunt Antónia Garcia, who had helped our family so much in those difficult days. Life had to continue on in another distant city.

Everything we had was very carefully loaded into a rented truck. My father, my mother holding her youngest daughter Sarah in her arms, and the driver rode in the truck's cab. All the other children travelled in the back covered by a tarpaulin. We left 73rd Street, Vila Formosa, São Paulo, in the evening of January 16, 1951. We travelled all night, stopping several times, here and there, for a little rest. Next morning, we arrived at a city called Rolândia, located in the southern region of Brazil, in the State of Paraná, which was settled by German immigrants who named it after the medieval hero Roland, a symbol of freedom in Germany. The truck stopped at a gas service station, where we found a water tap on the wall of the snack bar. We all washed our faces and enjoyed water so fresh, clean and in abundance!

There was a great bustle of trucks travelling in both directions, which I had never seen before, not even in São Paulo. So many trucks, carrying all kinds of products! We went into the small snack bar and drank coffee with milk and ate bread with butter, a typical Brazilian breakfast. It was delicious! Satisfied, we went back to the truck and our trip continued to the city of Mandaguaçu, which means Big Bee.[16] Even though it was a beautiful and hot sunny day, we had to be under the tarpaulin cover, because it was not allowed to carry people in the body of the truck, although many did. The police never caught us!

By noon we arrived in Mandaguaçu. The truck stopped in front of Garcia's Tailoring shop. My father got out of the truck; we all followed him. He went to look for my brother Antonio, who lived in the back of the workshop in a small rented apartment. He was married and, to our surprise, a beautiful boy had just been born that morning. He was named Valdeci Fernandes. He was my parents' first grandson, and my first nephew. In spite of being very tired we were all very happy!

After a while my brother Antonio arrived. We ran towards him and embraced him. He was very happy to see all of us. He took us to the small house he had rented for us, in the upper city, where we lived for a short time. The house was located in front of a large coffee plantation. It had enough rooms for all of us. God was good; He was ahead of us! It didn't take too long before my father, with the help of my brothers Samuel and Daniel, bought several lots on Batista Ribas Street and built a large house where we lived for many years.

As soon as we arrived in Big Bee, Samuel and Daniel started working at Garcia's Tailoring shop. There was a lot of work! When I was twelve, I also learned the trade and worked every day after school.

My father opened a grocery store where he sold fruits, vegetables, seeds, coffee plants and even sweets. During the years we lived in Mandaguaçu, that was his work. He loved it and was very happy. He had many friends in that city and trusted them. Sometimes it happened that he got somewhat tired and dozed off in the grocery store. People came to buy this or that and, as he was sleeping, didn't

---

[16] Mandaguaçu is an indigenous word that means Big Bee.

disturb him, got what they needed, left the money on the counter and went home. Sometimes we made jokes about it with him. He never minded!

That town was not always called Mandaguaçu. When we arrived there, it was, for a short time, called "Cala a Boca" which means "Shut Up," a pejorative term to designate a violent town. If a fight started and someone was killed and you saw it, then you had to shut up; otherwise you might eventually be killed too, and the situation would become worse. It was also called "Vila Guaíra"; however, a plebiscite was held November 14, 1951, to vote for a new name. The residents of the town chose Mandaguaçu, which is a Tupí-Guaraní word meaning Big Bee, because there were many beehives around the town, with thousands of honey bees. After World War II many immigrants from Italy bought land around the town that was very good for coffee plantations. The Italians worked very hard to establish themselves on the land, and in a short time they were producing and exporting coffee to Europe. They also needed people to work for them; so many Brazilians from the northeast of Brazil moved to Mandaguaçu. They travelled by a truck called "Pau de Arara"[17] for several days. It was a busy town in those days! Coffee trees surrounded it in all directions.

I lived in Mandaguaçu with my family – parents, brothers and sisters – until I was sixteen. To get some money I did all kinds of work – shining shoes, selling fruits and vegetables door to door, working in a clothing shop and finally, at the age of twelve, learning tailoring. I made trousers for men in my brother's tailor shop. Another tailor called Joãozinho tied my fingers for me to get used to a tailor's needle, the smallest needle on the market. He separated the parts of the trousers and taught me how to start. After a few trials I was a good tailor!

The junior high school moved to a new building in front of the town square, when I was in my first year. In those days we had Latin classes. Our teacher was an Italian missionary in the Capuchin Order,

---

[17] *Pau de Arara* is a Portuguese term that literarily means "macaw's perch." The term originates from the habit of tying birds to a pole for sale, where they also hang for transportation. It also refers to an irregular flat bed truck used to transport migrant workers.

the local Catholic church's priest. I often saw him walking up and down on the dusty streets of Mandaguaçu. He was always dressed in a brown priest's cassock and wore Capuchin sandals, but no socks! One day this priest went to the office of the principal in the junior high school, Miss Marilda Beltrane, and told her that I should be expelled from the school. I was not supposed to study there. The reason, he told her, was that I was a Protestant, and my family belonged to the Baptist church, and that school was only for Catholics, even though it was a public school. It was an order coming from him, the local Catholic priest.

The principal called me to her office and told me what the priest had said. She was somewhat embarrassed because she knew she should not forbid anyone to study. In those days the Catholic priest, in a small town, with a large Italian community, had a lot of power and influence, and his word in some cases was final.

My answer was that I was going to talk to my parents and brothers. They were furious! My eldest brother, Antonio, went to the town hall and asked for an appointment with the mayor, Dr. Arahy Ferreira. I went with him to talk to the mayor and explained to him what was happening at the junior high school, that the local priest did not want me to study there because I was a Protestant. Dr. Arahy was very surprised and asked us to be calm; he was going to resolve the situation, and I would continue studying. It didn't take too long before the Capuchin priest was no longer the Latin teacher. He was replaced by a Presbyterian pastor who travelled every week from another city, Maringá. I continued studying, completing junior high in November 1958.

The Capuchin missionary continued walking around the town, dressed in his brown cassock and sandals, without socks. He continued his program of trying to destroy the Protestant churches in our town, especially our Baptist church. Several times he sent the Catholic Marians to walk in front of our church and throw stones at the building. He also asked the Italian community to find Protestant Bibles and books in order to burn them in front of the Catholic church. I saw this happen a few times, as our house was close to that church.

After many years, on a return visit to Mandaguaçu I was very impressed with the changes that had occurred in the town. The same square, in front of the São Sebastião Catholic Church, where Bibles and evangelical books were burnt, is a beautiful place called Praça da

Bíblia (Bible Square). Where in the past Bibles had been burnt, today, reading is encouraged. Big Bee brought the Bible back to her people.

Inauguration of the Big Bee Baptist Church in August 1955

The Baptist church was a wooden building built at the end of Munhoz da Rocha Avenue, the main street in town. The location was not the best as there was great erosion very close to the church building. So, the members decided to sell the building and move near to downtown. My parents, my brothers and the Constantinov family gathered the resources and bought a piece of land close to the local cinema, where a new building was erected. The inauguration was on the first of August, 1955. It was a great blessing of God to the small Baptist community in town.

At the end of my final year of junior high school only five students finished the four-year course. In those days to get into junior high school a student had to pass an entrance exam. I had to study very hard to get in. I passed, studied for four years and, in the end, I received my diploma, in a graduation ceremony at the Cine Brazil.

I always had my adventures. I was a natural leader! A group of friends enjoyed playing soccer, but the school would not provide a ball for us to play with at the lunch break. Someone was designated each day to bring a ball made of socks with paper inside. One day, as we did not have a real soccer ball, I suggested the wonderful idea that all of us who played should bring some money and we would buy a real ball, a size five, good ball, like the ones used in a professional match. Everyone agreed and next day we brought some money, went and bought that beautiful size five, professional soccer ball. I brought it to the field of play and it rolled so marvelously, with screams from every student watching the match. We were very excited, but I did not have permission from the principal, Miss Marilda Beltrane, to buy a ball, much less to bring one to school!

One day when we were playing, with the ball rolling and a lot of screams – everyone happy – the principal came out of her office and the ball stopped rolling. Total silence! She asked for the ball and, to our sadness and surprise, she confiscated it and then asked who had had this wonderful idea to bring a ball to school. "Whose ball was it?"

This beautiful ball had been bought by all of us; we all gave some money to buy it, and some with sacrifice. "It belongs to all of us, because all contributed for it," I answered with a profound feeling of surprise, I was not expecting this reaction from the principal.

She took the ball to her office and asked me to accompany her. In her office she explained to me that I was not supposed to raise money to buy a ball. And then she gave me an assignment – to write fifty times, "I should not raise money to buy a soccer ball or play at break time." Our happiness ended there, but she later gave us back the ball and we started coming to the school to play in the afternoons, when there were no classes, in the *ginásio estadual* (state secondary school) of Mandaguaçu.

The principal understood that we could not be without sports and encouraged other sports. Volleyball became very popular in Mandaguaçu and other cities. A team was organized, and I started training with the junior high school group. We played at an improvised volleyball court made by the students. Once more I was speaking and asking questions. "Why don't we ask the city to build an official volleyball court for us?"

This time the suggestion was well accepted by the principal, and a committee was formed to talk to the mayor, Dr. Arahy Ferreira, asking for an official volleyball court. It didn't take too long for the court to be built, and we were all very happy. Almost every weekend we had a game against a team from another city. I was never the best, but I always had a place on our Big Bee team. Sometimes I played and sometimes I was on the bench.

Junior high school volleyball team, Big Bee, Paraná, Brazil

Alfaiataria Garcia (Garcia's Tailoring) was well known in town and in other towns. Many Italians, who moved from Italy after World War II to the towns around Mandaguaçu, bought land from the Companhia Melhoramentos Norte do Paraná (North Paraná Betterment Company) to plant coffee. My father, with the help of my brothers Antonio, Samuel and Daniel, bought some land as well and planted coffee. My father planted ten thousand coffee trees, and for a while had a very good profit from the selling of coffee. Some Italian families visited Italy every year and, before they left, they would buy new suits that were made by Garcia's Tailoring. There was always a lot of work! Sometimes we had to work all night in order to fill the orders.

When I finished at junior high school, I decided to move to São Paulo, where I had lived when I was a child. This time I was going alone. In those days Petrobras, the Brazilian petroleum company, was advertising on the radio for young people to study geology so that they might be employed by the company. At that time, the president of

Brazil, Dr. Getúlio Vargas,[18] was making speeches, talking about "the oil is ours." This was my goal! I wanted to go to São Paulo to continue studying to be a geologist and then go to work with Petrobras in the Amazon, where they were discovering oil.

---

[18] Dr. Getúlio Vargas was President from 1930-1934 and 1951-1954. On August 24, 1954, he killed himself in the midst of a political crisis.

6

&

DIFFERENT WAYS

*"The great use of life is to spend it
for something that will outlast it"
– William James*

It was very important for my parents that their children should study. They moved from a coffee plantation to town so that their children could go to school. When we moved to Mandaguaçu the first thing they did was to register me and my sisters at the public school, which was located in an old wooden building, divided into several classes to accommodate many new students who were coming to town. Some years later it was moved to a new building in front of the main square on land donated by one of its oldest inhabitants, an Italian immigrant by the name of Santo Carraro who established himself with his family in Mandaguaçu.

I was registered in Grade 2, as I had done Grade 1 in Lavínia, before moving to São Paulo, where I couldn't be registered. I always had the conviction that I wanted to study all my life. I told my parents that I would continue studying for many years.

As soon as I started school, I made several friends, boys and girls. However, one of the boys, whom I knew very well, was always bullying me, making jokes or pushing me here and there, besides intruding in my conversations with other students. One day he called me for a fight! I accepted the challenge and went at him so furiously that I gave him a *paliza*[19]. We were surrounded by a group of school students all shouting "Fight, fight!" We rolled on the ground, such was my rage in that moment, **the** moment of the day! I gave him a great beating! That boy never disturbed me again. Since that day, whenever he saw me, he would turn somewhere else looking for other boys like him, who also enjoyed bullying.

Somewhat sad, I walked along the school street, going to downtown. A girl about my age came to walk with me, as she saw I was upset because of the fight. I always liked to talk to Dora, a beautiful and wonderful girl. That day I really wanted to talk to someone who could understand me, and she did. Our friendship continued for many years.

In those days, when we finished primary school, we had to pass an entrance examination to move into junior high school. Almost every day I was looking for her. In the school or outside, even at her house, I was always anxious to see her and spend some time just talking. I never forgot when she waved her hand and called me by my name. A special feeling was becoming part of my life. At sunset I would sit on a bench in the square in front of her house waiting for her to come out, and then I would come to greet her and stay for a while conversing.

"Hi, Dora? How are you? You are beautiful!" It was a special moment.

"Everything is great! And you, João Garcia?"

And we continued talking, especially about school. "The biology teacher is very demanding. He gives us too much homework!"

We did not have too much "news" to talk about, so our conversation was mainly about school, family and friends. In this pioneer town surrounded by coffee plantations, the main source of income, many families had come from different areas of Brazil and also from Europe, mainly Italy. They all were looking for the "green gold" as coffee was known.

---

[19] *Paliza* is a word in the Spanish language that means "a spanking, a beating."

Her father also would come out and sit on a small bench in front of the house, and I would greet him, "Good afternoon, Dr. Dimas."

He was a polite and distinguished gentleman involved in the community. Still I knew it was time to leave; so I would get moving. "*Tchau*, Dora, see you tomorrow at school."

I had a world of imagination going on inside my mind. We were two teenagers who did not know too much about life. Dora was a beautiful girl, rather sweet, polite, with several other boys interested in her as a girlfriend. There was always someone who would invite her to go out to the movies or just for a stroll in the local central square. It was the time when boys and girls would go out on summer evenings for a "footing"[20] on the central square. I was the last in the list of many! However, I didn't care; I was always looking for her and, when we met, I felt in the clouds. It was wonderful!

We had been friends since I was ten years old; we studied at the same school and were in the same class. Our friendship was becoming serious! After a long conversation I asked her to be my girlfriend. I said, "I love you." I really didn't know what she was thinking. She did not give me an answer at that moment. However, a few days later she gave me a positive answer. I was very happy and radiant with joy!

"João Garcia," as she always called me, "let's go out together, talk and get to know each other better. If God approves this, we will follow His direction." Dora was very religious since she accepted Jesus as her Saviour, visiting a Seventh Day Adventist Church. She always talked about her life as a Christian and her future following Jesus.

Her family had moved from Bastos, in the State of São Paulo, where there was a large community of Japanese immigrants. Her father, Dr. Dimas da Silva Rocha, a dentist, had been mayor from 1948 to 1951. Finishing his mandate, he moved with his family to Mandaguaçu, where he established himself and became involved in

---

[20] Footing, an English Portuguese word in the fifties and sixties refers, to boys and girls walking a short distance in the city square talking to each other, finding a girlfriend or boyfriend.

the life of the town. He was the first dentist, a town councilor and, once, Town Chairman.

When I finished junior high school in November 1958, my goal was to continue studying. I always thought that, if I studied, I would have a good job. I didn't want to live all my life in Big Bee. In my thoughts I aimed for university. It looked like an impossibility, but, in my mind, I could think, imagine, have goals, dream big and not give up.

It was at this time that I received an invitation from my brother-in-law Euclides and my sister Carmen to go to São Paulo and live with them to continue my studies. In Mandaguaçu there was no high school. If I wanted to continue studying, I had to move either to Maringá, which was not too far, or to São Paulo. I accepted the invitation of my brother-in-law and sister. I was trained as a tailor; so I could work and study. I wanted to be a geologist and, if possible, to work with Petrobras, the great Brazilian state petroleum company. In those days there was an advertisement on the radio that was often broadcast encouraging young people to study geology and get a job with Petrobras. Every day I heard the words from our president, Getúlio Vargas, saying, "the oil is ours." In his speeches he was emphatic that nobody would take our petroleum. There used to be some countries that wanted to explore for petroleum in the Amazon and in the Northeast of Brazil. It was President Getúlio Vargas who sanctioned, on October 3, 1953, the 2004 law that started Petrobras, which was recruiting young people to work with them. I wanted to be one of these young men. I was ready to take on the Scientific Course[21], which was preparation for an undergraduate Geology Degree at the university. Then I left for São Paulo.

Dora entered Normal School; after that she was accepted for the B.A. program at the university in Mandaguari, a city not too far from Mandaguaçu, and then she accepted an invitation to be a French teacher at the local public (state) high school, the *ginásio*. For many years she was a remarkable teacher in that school. Once, she needed a record of the French national anthem, "La Marseillaise," sung by a choir. I went to a record company, bought one and sent it to her.

---

[21] The Scientific Course was the same as high school but with emphasis in science. It took me five years to finish it. It was a long walk in the same direction.

Even though I moved to São Paulo I had Dora in my heart. I always thought of her. I was grateful because I had met her and she had become my girlfriend. She became part of my life. I loved her so much! At a distance we talked by letter. Every week I went to the secretary's box at the Colégio Batista Brasileiro (Brazilian Baptist School) to pick up the letter she had sent me. And then I would sit on one of the garden benches of the school beside the Faculdade Teológica Batista (Baptist Seminary) and slowly read her letter. She talked about being far from me and about family, friends, church and small town news and finished with hugs and kisses. I always immediately answered her letters with love.

I travelled back to Mandaguaçu every summer. Some years had passed and I was in my last year of the Scientific Course. I was getting ready for the seminary. By this time, I already knew that I was not going to be a geologist. God had called me to the pastoral ministry. I had received a firm conviction that He wanted me as a pastor in a Baptist church, and not in a petroleum field of Petrobras. As soon as I finished the Scientific Course, I would register myself in the São Paulo Faculdade Teológica Batista, to take the Bachelor of Theology.[22]

It was then that an issue arose between Dora and me. We had to talk about what was most important in our lives, our Christian faith. She belonged to the Seventh Day Adventist Church and I belonged to the Baptist Church. Every time I travelled to Mandaguaçu to see her we always talked about these two ways of living the Christian faith.

In January of 1965 Dora came to visit me in São Paulo. Her brother Delcir came with her. They stayed at my mother's house in Parque São Lucas. We had a lot of time to talk. It was a joyful and happy time. Every day we went out to visit several places in São Paulo. We also visited the Brazilian Baptist School, the Baptist Seminary and the Seventh Day Adventist School, where we spent a Saturday. On her last Sunday we attended a service at the Perdizes

---

[22] The Scientific Course took me five years to finish and the Bachelor of Theology another five years. So, I spent ten years in São Paulo, studying and working. I was so grateful to God that He had always been with me, showing me His ways, leading me in His paths and guiding me in His truth.

Baptist Church, where I was a member and assistant to Pastor Alberto Blanco de Oliveira. In the afternoon we went for lunch in a local restaurant and spent the afternoon at Parque da Água Branca. We talked for a long time about our different churches.

Our thoughts about our faith had common points and different points. We both believed in Jesus Christ. For us the Bible was the book where we found teaching and guidance for our Christian life. We also believed in doing good works and community service because we were Christians; Jesus taught us that.

But there were a few different teachings that were getting between us and had to be discussed. For us Baptists, the law was temporary, the pedagogue, the educator.[23] Jesus made a new alliance with us, based on His blood poured out on the cross. With the resurrection of Jesus, a new way of worshipping was taught by his disciples. The day of worship began to be Sunday, the first day of the week, and not Saturday, the seventh day. Dora was always saying to me that we could worship in her church on Saturdays and in my Baptist church on Sundays. Maybe this could be done if I were a lay person and not a Baptist pastor.

Another very important doctrine was the belief of the Seventh Day Adventists that, when a person dies, his soul stays in the tomb until the coming of Jesus, when the person will be resurrected. These different views were taking us far away from each other. I loved Dora, but it became painful!

I wanted her to move to São Paulo, to be close to me, so we could discuss these issues more often. But for her to move to São Paulo, live at the Baptist School, continue her studies at the university and become a member of a Baptist church was an impossibility. Besides, she was already a French teacher at the local secondary school, even though she had not finished her Bachelor of Education. Her parents suggested to me that, as soon as I finished my studies at the Faculdade Teológica Batista, I go back to Mandaguaçu and become a teacher too. In a small town there is always a need for another teacher! I was grateful that they were caring for me, but I could not accept their suggestion because I had a different goal. I had

---

[23] Galatians 3.21-29 "the Law was in charge of us until Christ came..." v.24, I Cor. 10, Hebrews 9.

a firm conviction of my call to the ministry and I could not make a change and go back to Mandaguaçu.

Dora and I prayed a lot about these issues. It was our future that we were discussing, and a decision had to be made. I wanted her happiness above all, and it seemed impossible under these conditions to make her happy. God was guiding my life in another direction. Sadness took over my heart, but at the same time I felt that, for her happiness, it would be better to end what I most desired, to continue at her side.

One day, after a sleepless night, I sat on a bench in the Baptist Seminary, looking into the distance through the window, thinking of Dora, with the greatest sadness and heartache, but I wrote her a letter stating the reasons why we had to end our relationship. It was a very difficult decision, but I knew that God was guiding my future. I was not alone, never alone. A "big bee" always flies high looking for a place where it would be happy. I wanted her to fly with me and be happy. I always desired her happiness. But with different thoughts, goals and ideas it was impossible to accomplish it, to make her happy.

She wrote back expressing her disappointment, sadness and surprise. But at the crossroads we had to follow different ways. She continued being a French teacher in Mandaguaçu, in the State of Paraná, and I followed my call to the ministry. God had many surprises for me in my future.

CALL AND PREPARATION

7

&

THE GOOD SAMARITAN

*"When you help someone, it does make a difference.
And how it does!"*

One sunny morning in January 1959, I left the town of Mandaguaçu (Big Bee), in the State of Paraná, Brazil. I was sixteen years old and I had lived there since I was nine years old. Mandaguaçu was a small town. I left to go to São Paulo, the largest city in Brazil, more than a thousand kilometres away. My goal was to continue studying. All I wanted was to go to university in the future.

When I finished junior high school, the principal of the state secondary school of Mandaguaçu, Miss Marilda Beltrane, asked me about my dreams for the future. I answered her that I was going to São Paulo to continue studying.

"João, it is going to be very difficult for you. In São Paulo the schools are very expensive."

She was only alerting me about the difficulties that I would certainly face in a big city. I listened and thanked her, but my determination was to continue studying.

"I am going to work to pay for my expenses," I explained to her. I had a profession, I was a tailor, and I would find a place where I could work and go to school in the evenings.

We left very early in the morning. My father walked silently beside me. He was sad because I was leaving, and we did not know what was waiting for me in the big city. We walked along the trail through the bushes beside our house towards the town centre. We passed in front of our Baptist church, reached the Garcia's Tailoring shop, where I worked with my brothers, and arrived at the small bus station on the main square downtown. The Mandaguaçu secondary school, on the other side of the square, reminded me of the wonderful time I had spent there, studying, playing soccer and volleyball and kidding with my friends.

The bus arrived, stopped beside the sidewalk and some passengers got off. I took my luggage to be put on the luggage rack. My father gave me some last instructions and we bid each other farewell, as the driver had a break and a coffee. The bus was coming from another city called Paranávaí and the destination was Londrina, with a stop in Maringá. I took a seat beside the window. The trip was starting. Through the window, pensive, I saw the garden where many times I had met my friends, boys and girls, to talk about so many things. Next the bus turned the corner and we were passing in front of my father's grocery store, the Garcia's Tailoring shop and the land on which the Baptist church had its first building. I remembered when, in my childhood, I belonged to the Sunday school, assisted with the services, participated in the Christmas pageant and attended the prayer meetings every Wednesday.

I always went with my parents and sisters to the evening services. In those long-gone days there was no electricity in the town. I went in front carrying the lamp, walking along a shortcut behind the church building. On the dark winter nights, when the wind was blowing cold, my mother would shout, "Put your finger on your belly button so the lamp does not go out." My mother's superstition!

Continuing my trip on the bus, we passed in front of the Constantinov family's sawmill. They were a wonderful family, members of our Baptist church and very faithful to God. Our families built the church building that was close to the movie theater, Cine Brazil. It became quite easy for us to go to the movies on Sunday evenings! After the service some of us went to watch a good movie, which was a novelty. The theatre came to town in the early fifties. The only problem was that those who liked to gossip were always looking for things to criticize, people like our neighbour; every time she saw me in the theatre, knowing that my mother did not like me to go to Cine Brazil, she would run before I came home and tell my mother that she saw me there. Then it was a big problem and my mother would spank me with a rod!

"I told you not to go to the movie."

I would tell her to prepare a stronger rod for next Sunday!

In those days going to the movies was a big sin. At the Sunday service we were told many times, by the local or visiting preacher, that sin includes going to Cine Brazil.

Years later, my Mom came to live with us for a while. She enjoyed watching the soap operas, "the Brazilian novellas," which are morally worse than the Roy Rogers movies that we watched in the fifties. Every afternoon she asked me to turn on the TV, so that she could watch "the novellas."

I joked with her, saying, "Watching novellas is a big sin."

She laughed and would say again, "It's time for the novella; please, turn on the TV."

I then turned on the TV and she stayed there watching, until the national news came on.

The small town of Mandaguaçu was left behind. The road that took us to Maringá was dusty and bumpy. It went through a large coffee plantation. Those days coffee was known as the "green gold" of Brazil. Trucks passed, day and night, full of sacks and sacks of coffee whose destination was the port of Paranaguá, in the State of Paraná, and from there they were exported to Europe.

Many times, on those coffee plantations, my friends and I went on Sunday afternoons to pick up watermelons, like stealing! One Sunday as we were sitting on the ground and eating a watermelon, the owner of that coffee plantation just appeared from nowhere with a shotgun and shouted in a very loud voice, "You thieves run away right now, or I will shoot you! Shameless kids."

We ran fast, each one of us in a different direction, some shouting and some crying! What a day! I have never forgotten.

We passed the small village of Iguatemi and didn't take long to arrive at old Maringá, where some passengers got off. I stayed on the bus until it stopped at the new Maringá bus station. I got off, carrying my bag, and walked slowly to the train station, bought my first-class ticket to São Paulo, entered a coach, took a seat and waited silently for the train's departure. It was the beginning of a long trip, more than a thousand kilometres by train to São Paulo. A new and unknown life was ahead of me. I had many thoughts in my mind. How would the trip be? How about the arrival at my sister's home? Where would I find a job and a high school? At the same time, I prayed, asking God to be with me and guide my life. I believed that He had something special for me. I was never alone. I then said a verse from the Bible that I knew by heart, "He will give you the desires of your heart. Commit your way to the LORD; trust in him, and he will act" (Psalm 37:4b-5).

The train left at noon. It was an old train but the best there was in those days. It arrived from São Paulo the night before and returned at noon the following day. The engine, pulling the carriages, left Maringá, the new part of the city, and then the subdivision, Vila Operária, where the First Baptist Church was located, which we had visited many times coming from Mandaguaçu for special celebrations. It didn't take too long to arrive in Marialva and then continue to Apucarana and Londrina. The old train, smoking, whistling and roaring, continued noisily on its journey. It crossed the Paranápanema River, entering the State of São Paulo. We arrived at Ourinhos about ten o'clock in the evening. It was very dark. At this station we had to wait a long time for another train that was coming from Alta Paulista. As soon as it arrived many got on and our journey continued.

I was tired from travelling all day, just looking through the window at so many coffee plantations. I slept, thinking about what my life would be like in the big city. I woke up in the morning arriving in Sorocaba, an industrial city, in those days well known as the Manchester of Brazil[24], referring to the English industrial city. In this city I had some friends from Mandaguaçu who were studying at a private boarding school. It was a Methodist school for boys and girls. Rich people from Mandaguaçu sent their children to this school as it was a very good and respectable school. The train didn't stop very

---

[24] *Unicamp* news article "How Sorocaba Became a Paulista Manchester"

long in Sorocaba and we soon left. It was the last part of our long and memorable journey.

Soon I could see that we were coming into São Paulo. It was a January day in 1959. The train stopped at the Luz Station[25], where the passengers got up quickly, as if they were worried about losing their next connection, or maybe they were tired of sitting for so long and anxious to get off. They took their bags, rushing, almost trampling each other. That day I felt like a bee far from the hive, looking for a new place where I could rest, but always trusting that God was guiding my flying. I was not flying alone! I had learned to trust in God.

I stayed there quietly just looking at the people and waiting for everything to calm down. Then I calmly rose, took my only bag and slowly left the station. The street was very busy. Cars and people in all directions! I took a taxi and asked the driver to take me to Vila Formosa, the address written on my small piece of paper. After going along many busy streets, we arrived in front of a very modest house where my sister and brother-in-law Carmen and Euclides lived. I paid the taxi driver and knocked on the door. Carmen was waiting for me; Euclides was working. I was very happy to meet my sister and to be back in São Paulo. I had come back to Vila Formosa! I came alone as a "big bee" looking for a place to build its hive and not ever go back.

It was a new beginning in the biggest city of Brazil. I brought a heart full of hope and will to succeed. I drank a delicious coffee prepared by my sister, rested for a while, and that same day went looking for a job. I wanted to work but also to study. I had to look for a job because my parents could not pay for my education. My sister and brother-in-law gave me room and board. I had to do my part. They were the "Good Samaritan" of the parable told by Jesus as recorded in Luke 10:25-37. I have always been so grateful to them!

I walked up Saigon Street to the centre of Vila Formosa, going into every tailor's workshop I could find. I was looking for a job as a tailor. I knew how to make trousers, as I learned at my brother's tailoring shop in Mandaguaçu. Those days it was an excellent job as shops were not yet selling "ready-made" suits. People would go to a

---

[25] *Wikipedia*, under the words Luz Station, "The Luz Station is the common name for a railway station in the Luz neighbourhood in São Paulo, Brazil. The station is part of the metropolitan rail system run by CPTM."

tailor to have their suits tailor-made. Some even wanted them "hand-made"! So, tailor's workshops were everywhere. It didn't take too long before two of them offered me a job. I took the one that was closer to my sister's home, on Eduardo Cotching Avenue, in front of Sampaio Vidal Square. I was only sixteen years old but accustomed to work. Every day I would walk to the tailor workshop and make a pair of trousers!

Carmen and Euclides

I wanted to register myself in the Scientific Course. I was planning to be a geologist and get a job with Petrobras, the Brazilian petroleum company. I needed help to find schools in a big city like that. Where could I find a school close to Vila Formosa? My cousin Josué offered to help me. He was born in São Paulo, and knew the city quite well and where some schools where located. He worked at a bank downtown. Using the telephone book, he wrote down the names of some schools that offered the Scientific Course – Colégio Sarmento in Brás, Colégio Estadual in Mooca and Colégio Coronel Paulo Egídio de Oliveira Carvalho in Vila Maria. All these schools are free government schools where students didn't have to pay for their education. We went to all these schools enquiring about a vacancy for a new student. Col. Paulo Egídio de Oliveira Carvalho, Vila Maria, accepted all my documents and asked me to wait while they checked them. I was a little bit suspicious that I was not going to be accepted having come from a distant interior town.

It took too long. I had to make a decision because it was close to the time when schools in Brazil started a new school year. So, I opted to go to a private school close to Vila Formosa. It was called Colégio Rui Barbosa on Prazeres Street, which is parallel to Catumbi Street, a well-known street in Brás. I registered myself and started school. A few months later I was informed by letter that I had been accepted at the state high school Col. Paulo Egídio de Oliveira Carvalho, Vila Maria. I transferred to that school even though it was farther from Vila Formosa, where I was living. And as the course was in the evening from 7 to 11 p.m. I could work during the day. It took two buses to get there but I was very happy.

I studied at that school for three years. As I came from the interior, where schooling is not as good as in a big city like São Paulo, I had to do the first year twice. I failed my first attempt but did not give up! At this time, I was no longer working as a tailor. I found a job in an office in the centre of São Paulo, on the sixth floor at 195 Direita Street, with a company called Cal Itu SA. They made whitewash used for painting, and sold cement and iron for construction. I started as an office boy[26]. Later, as I liked to talk, I presume, they offered me a position as a salesman. I also had the responsibility of debt collection. I was very happy and accepted the position. I had the opportunity of travelling all over São Paulo and at the same time I could study when I was on a bus or train. It was a good and very profitable time, and I also earned much more money.

One day I was doing my work in the Jewish area of São Paulo, on José Paulino Street, Bom Retiro. I had to go to a condo to collect some money from a Jewish man and sell him more of our products. I knocked at the door; he opened it, asked me to come in and sit at a table, offered me something to drink and treated me very, very well. He also talked to me for a few minutes, asking about who I was, my family and what I was doing in a big city like São Paulo. I answered that I had come to São Paulo from the State of Paraná because I

---

[26] The phrase office-boy is still used in Brazil for someone who helps in the office.

wanted to continue studying. He congratulated me for the goals I had for my life, to work and to study.

"That is what many young people do in São Paulo," he said.

Then he proceeded to pay the debt owed to the company I worked for and placed a good order for steel and lime. He said he wanted me to have a good commission that month. Probably without knowing, that man was also a Good Samaritan who was encouraging and teaching me to do the same for others as he did for me.

I always had to collect debts from companies that owed Cal Itu SA. I carried with me documents that I had to give to those who paid in full. I travelled by bus, by train, by tram and on foot. Many times, I arrived home very tired, had my dinner quickly and went to night school, taking two buses to get there. One company close to Praça da Sé (Sé Square) in the centre of São Paulo owed Cal Itu some money, wanted to pay and wanted to buy some more materials. It was a well-known construction company in São Paulo. I went to their office with the document, but the person responsible for paying wasn't there. I was supposed to be back the next day. I left and never went back, forgetting the document in my pocket!

One day when I arrived for work in the office, Senhor Lineu, one of the partners in Cal Itu SA, called me into his office and asked me, "What happened to the document for that construction company from which you went to collect?"

I was very silent! I had a red face! I went to my desk, looked in my coat and there it was, the document. I went back to Senhor Lineu's office, showed him the document and told him where I had found it. I had forgotten to go back to collect the money from that construction company. He was not really angry because he knew me and liked my work, but he said, "The engineer in charge of the construction company called me, asking about the document. He is very angry, asking me to fire you."

Senhor Lineu was sad that he had to let me go because that company was a good customer and Cal Itu could not afford to lose them. So, he proceeded to fire me and gave me a very "good package." A few years later I understood that even in that situation God was leading me. I had to go somewhere else; a "big bee" never stays on only one flower!

The money I received from Cal Itu SA was a good amount, and I was very happy to give it all to my sister Carmen and brother-in-law Euclides to start the construction of their modest house. They were very happy and thankful. They put it together with their savings and built the house in Parque São Lucas where they lived for many years.

The youth group of Vila Formosa Baptist Church organized special meetings Saturday evenings. A guest speaker was invited to bring the message. In one of these meetings a well-known preacher in São Paulo, Rev. Eliezer Pereira de Barros, came to preach. He challenged the young people to dedicate their lives to the pastoral ministry. I listened very carefully. While I was listening, I was also paying attention to what God was saying to me. I was trying to understand what the message was. Does God want me in the ministry? As a pastor? This was in my mind all the time I was listening to the message. It touched me profoundly at that moment. I thought that my life was changing. No more thinking about geology and work with Petrobras. God wanted me to follow Him in another direction. I was the first to answer the preacher's appeal.

From that moment on, my future was unknown. God was in command and He was certainly guiding me in the right direction. I also decided not to work full-time anymore. I had to find a part-time job and dedicate myself entirely to study. God then led me to a missionary called Rev. Robert Cunningham, from Canada. He was the editor of an evangelical newspaper called *The Herald*. I learned that he was looking for a young man to work part-time at his office. The work was to organize the distribution of the paper to the churches and to take the parcels to the central post office to be sent to subscribers.

I continued studying at the state high school Col. Paulo Egídio de Oliveira Carvalho in Vila Maria. Sometimes some students, including me, would miss some classes to go to the local theater to listen to Dr. Jânio Quadros, a presidential candidate, and João Goulart, his running mate, two populist politicians. Jânio promised to wipe out the corruption in Brazil! He had a broom in his hands as a symbol of his promise. He won the election, but was president for just a few months. He said that he could not continue because there were strong "hidden forces" opposing his presidency. He left, and the vice-president, João Goulart, took over.

I was not doing very well at school, in the Scientific Course. The problem was that the school in Madaguaçu was not as good as the one in São Paulo. We did not have local teachers for mathematics and Portuguese. The teachers had to come from another city, and they came once a month. We were self-taught. The teacher came and gave us homework for a month; we had to study by ourselves and take a test every time he returned. I always passed my tests but didn't learn very much. So, in São Paulo I had to study extra hours. I did the first year twice!

At Vila Maria I started typing lessons. Every evening at six o'clock I studied for about an hour. I thought that they might help me in the future. In those days typing was very important. I worked until five o'clock at Cal Itu SA, took a bus from downtown São Paulo, arrived at the typing school by six, studied for about one hour and then went to school from seven to eleven. It was like a marathon! When I think about those days, I remember how difficult it was; however, I was very happy with the wonderful opportunity to prepare myself for finishing my Scientific Course and to learn typing, preparing myself to go to the seminary to study for the ministry. I was following God's direction.

At the Vila Alpina Baptist Church, where my family were members, I met a young man who worked and lived at the Colégio Batista Brasileiro (Brazilian Baptist School)[27], in the subdivision of Perdizes. He told me that the school was looking for someone to work and live there. If I was interested, I should go there and talk to the principal, Rev. Werner Kaschell. Maybe he would take me.

I took his advice seriously. One day I woke up early, had my breakfast and took the bus to the subdivision of Perdizes, to the Brazilian Baptist School. I walked up the steps in front of the school, came into a large hall, went to the secretary and asked for Rev. Werner Kaschell. Miss Fany told me that he was teaching, but he would see me after class. I waited in front of his office and, when he was available, he invited me into his office and asked, "How can we help you?"

"I have come from a city in the State of Paraná to São Paulo to study. My intention was to study geology at the university, but God changed my direction and is calling me into the ministry. I am looking for a part-time job so I can dedicate myself only to study. I met a

---

[27] Colégio Batista Brasileiro was founded in 1902 by Southern Baptist missionaries. Today it is a prestigious and large school in São Paulo.

young man at Vila Alpina Baptist Church who works here; his name is Osmar Gimenez. He told me that you are looking for someone to work and live at the school and I am interested," I answered.

"Yes, it is true; we are, and you can come today if you are available. We have a position in the area of discipline, and you will be assistant to Senhor Souza. We also have a room available for you. We offer you schooling with free accommodation; you can transfer your Scientific Course to us. You have to pay for your meals."

This was wonderful; God was leading the way! I went back to my sister's house, took my belongings and left for the Brazilian Baptist School. I was also offered some hours at the adjacent Faculdade Teológica Batista (Baptist Seminary). Dr. Thurmon Bryant, a Southern Baptist missionary, was looking for a part-time office secretary to type his letters and sermons. That was another blessing from God, Who was opening new horizons for me. I thanked God and recited the words of Psalm 91:1, "You who live in the shelter of the Most High... abide in the shadow of the Almighty."

In my last year of the Scientific Course I felt once again the hand of God leading me. When my friend Ary Veloso, a student at the Faculdade Teológica Batista, finished his studies, he was invited to go to study at the Dallas Theological Seminary. He had come from Belo Horizonte to study at the Baptist Seminary. We became very good friends. We were always together talking about soccer, studies, social problems and above all the Kingdom of God. At that time, he worked with Rev. Eneas Tognini, who was one of the leaders of the movement called "Spiritual Renewal." Ary lived in a small apartment at the back of Rev. Eneas Tognini's residence. Before moving to Dallas, he introduced me to Rev. Tognini and suggested that I take his position in the Spiritual Renewal Movement. I left the position at the Brazilian Baptist School, accepted the invitation from Rev. Eneas Tognini and moved to the small apartment at the back of his residence.

The Spiritual Renewal Movement influenced many Baptist churches in Brazil at that time. My work was as an assistant to Rev. Eneas Tognini. When he went to preach at churches in São Paulo, I would accompany him. Every Thursday I went with him to Sé Square, in the centre of São Paulo, where he preached to many. Sunday mornings I helped him on the half-hour radio program "Spiritual Renewal." As he was also a pastor at Perdizes Baptist Church I met with him in his office for prayer before the service, and also helped answer the letters he received every day. I was very happy to work beside a great man of God; however, I continued as assistant to Dr. Thurmon Bryant at the Baptist Seminary.

I was convinced that God had chosen me for that moment in my life. One day, however, in my last year of the Scientific Course, I woke up and noticed that I couldn't see from my right eye! It was the beginning of a troubling time in my life. I didn't know what to do! I had no medical insurance. For many days I was worried, asking myself what was happening. Why could I not see from my right eye? After many weeks without telling anybody about it, one evening, I went to the church for a prayer meeting and asked for prayer, explaining what was happening with my right eye.

After the prayer meeting, a person that I knew very well approached me and said, "The chaplain at the Hospital das Clínicas is my friend; I am going to call and tell him that 'there was a young man, in the prayer meeting tonight, who has a problem in his eye and has no medical insurance. Could you help?'"

The chaplain was a young Catholic priest! He answered, "Bring him here immediately and I will talk to the doctors who are on duty tonight."

We went immediately to the Hospital das Clínicas. When my friend and I arrived, there was a group of doctors waiting for me. After checking me, one of them said, "You have to come back here tomorrow morning and register yourself as a patient; your problem is very serious."

I thanked my friend and the chaplain very much. I knew that God was leading me and helping me. I was never alone. He was with me all the way. Next morning, I registered myself at the admitting office and for one year Dr. Kanto, a Korean ophthalmologist who lived in Brazil, took care of me. I had to go to that hospital every week, for many, many tests, antibiotics and vitamins.

One day, about a year later I went to see Dr. Kanto. After consultation he told me, "You were in danger of becoming completely blind in both eyes. We managed to save the left eye, and you should be very happy because 'in the land of the blind whoever has an eye is king.' From now on you are going to have a good life. Better one eye than none."

During all that time what I most wanted was to be healed. Many people were praying for me. Rev. Eneas Tognini prayed, laying his hands on me. I believed that God was listening to those prayers; He had a purpose for me. He was guiding me and it was not a disease that would prevent me from continuing to serve Him in the ministry he was preparing for me.

The healing happened one day when I was visiting my mother. I spent the night at her home and the next morning, when I woke up, to my surprise I saw everything around me with my two eyes. God had performed a great miracle in my life! Once again it was proof that He is powerful to do marvelous things in the lives of those who trust Him. I remembered the words I had read many times in the first epistle of Paul to his disciple Timothy, "I am grateful to Christ Jesus our Lord, who has strengthened me, because he judged me faithful and appointed me to his service" (1 Timothy 1:12). From that day forward, life continued as normal. Praise God that He touched my eye and I was healed!

8

&

REVOLUTION

*"Trust in the LORD with all your heart,
and do not rely on your own insight."*
– Proverbs 3:5

My father sold his house, the grocery store and the coffee plantation farm. My brother Daniel, who, by this time, had his own tailoring shop, sold it and his house. They combined their money, formed a partnership and moved to São Paulo. They built two small houses and one large hall where they opened a supermarket at Parque São Lucas. It was January 1963, one year before the military revolution.

After the death of President Getúlio Vargas on August 24, 1954, Dr. Juscelino Kubischeck was elected for five years in 1955. Dr. Jânio Quadros was elected president on January 31, 1961, and João Goulart elected vice-president. After Dr. Jânio Quadros renounced the presidency just seven months later on August 31, 1961, João Goulart became the president of Brazil on September 7, 1961. It was a very difficult time of uncertainty, changes, student clashes and strikes. Factories were closed, and many people lost their jobs. Many times, in downtown São Paulo, I saw students clashing with each other. The University of São Paulo had left-leaning tendencies, while the Mackenzie Presbyterian University was opposed to it; clashes happened quite often. The National Congress couldn't come to a satisfactory conclusion about what to do, nor could the president, who had socialist communist ideas and was supported by the unions and some political parties. So, at dawn on April 1, 1964, João Goulart was deposed by a military junta and taken to Uruguay, where he died on December 6, 1976. The junta was installed and governed Brazil until March 16, 1985.

It was very dangerous to live in São Paulo in those days. Thousands of communists were trying to take power. We did not know exactly who was and who wasn't a communist. Even your close friends could be among them. I worked with a friend at the Brazilian Baptist School who once called me to his house, showed me a rifle and tried to convince me that I should get one too, for, if there were a revolution, he would fight for the Communist Party. He was a member of the same Baptist church as I was. In São Paulo the most well-known communist leader was Carlos Marighella, a Marxist Brazilian writer, poet, politician and guerrilla fighter. He was against the military junta that had been installed in Brazil. He was killed by the DOPS (Department of Political and Social Order), the Brazilian secret police, November 4, 1969, on Casa Branca Boulevard in São Paulo. He was 57 years old.

At this time, I was a student at the Faculdade Teológica Batista and president of the students' academic centre. One day a young man came to see me. He was the president of the students' academic centre of the São Paulo State University. That centre was a member of the União Nacional dos Estudantes (National Union of Students) or UNE, with communist tendencies. We sat at a table and he began talking about that moment in Brazil's history. He mentioned that several evangelical theological academic centres had become members of UNE. The invitation was given to me to talk to our academic centre and discuss membership with the students and participation in the counter-revolution that was certainly coming.

I was totally against such an idea, and I also knew that the students of the Baptist Seminary would agree with me. I told that young man that we had no communist tendencies and, therefore, I would reject such an invitation. He then left, and I never heard of him again. At the next meeting of the academic centre I mentioned the visit of the student from São Paulo State University. I told the students that I had rejected the invitation. They all agreed with my decision and we voted not to become a member of UNE.

Those were difficult days! Thousands of people were investigated by the secret police (DOPS) who were suspicious of them being communists. Many were put in jail, many were tortured and others were killed. Some disappeared without a trace. In Mandaguaçu, friends of ours, including some from our Baptist church, were taken for interrogation and we never saw them again, even though they were not declared communists.

My father and my brother Daniel were, in their business, indirectly victims of the revolution. Many factories were closed. Some investors were from Europe or America. They were afraid of the future in Brazil. The supermarket that should have been such a good business became a bad dream. Several of their customers lost their jobs. There was no more money for food. When they came for groceries, they took only a little, barely enough to survive! It was not possible for my father and brother to continue with the supermarket without people shopping. I remember, when I went to visit them, seeing piles and piles of products that were not sold. Money was scarce those days! Bankruptcy was the only solution. Many other businesses closed their doors. In reality, it was a great revolution in our family!

In July 1964 I went with my father on a trip to the State of Paraná. Our plan was to visit Mandaguaçu, Cianorte and Umuarama. We arrived in Mandaguaçu and stayed with a family friend, Benizio Niza. He was the father-in-law of my brother Daniel. My father was anxious! We were returning to a city where he had been prosperous. He had had everything, a good business, a house and a coffee farm plantation. He had sold everything to open the supermarket in São Paulo! He had lost everything. The political revolution caused great upheaval in his life.

After a few days we continued our trip. Our next stop was Cianorte, where my brother Samuel and his family lived. He had moved from Mandaguaçu and opened his own tailoring shop. It was a rainy day! The roads were not paved and were very muddy. We took a bus to Maringá and from there another bus to Cianorte. We hadn't travelled too long when our bus got stranded. The back tires were in a hole and couldn't move. The driver called for help, but it would take a long time. We thirty passengers discussed the problem and came to the decision that we would not be able to continue unless we ourselves helped push the bus out of the muddy pothole. So, everybody got off, including my father. I asked him not to push because of his age. After a superb effort from everyone the bus came out and we could continue our journey even though we all were dirty! As we continued travelling, I noticed that my father was not well. His face looked very tired.

"Hijo, tengo dolores en mi pecho," he said in the Spanish language.

He was having pain in his chest. We arrived at my brother Samuel's home. He was the owner of Alfaiataria Garcia in Cianorte, a pioneering city in the north part of the State of Paraná.

That afternoon my father was feeling better. In the evening, however, the pain in his chest came back. It was very painful! He couldn't stop complaining; what a pain, all night! Next morning, we took him to the doctor, who said that we should not continue our trip, but return to São Paulo, to a hospital. We went back to São Paulo the same day by air. The flight was tranquil, but I could see in my father's face that he was not well. We arrived at the Congonhas Airport and went home by taxi. He went straight to bed and I called a doctor, who came immediately. After seeing him, he was very straight forward with us and said, "Your father has angina pectoris and he is not going to make it."

He gave him some medication to alleviate the pain, but repeated that, even if we took him to hospital, he would not make it. There was no heart surgery those days in Brazil.[28] Nevertheless, my brother and I took him to the nearest hospital. As my brother was paying the fee for the admission, a nurse and I took him on an emergency stretcher to a room. When we entered and were transferring him to a bed he died in my arms. My brother came in just a few minutes later and we both wept at the death of our father, a wonderful man who laboured all his life so that we could have enough to live a good life. Since he understood the message of the gospel, he and my mother were people of faith. The funeral was at Vila Alpina

---

[28] The first heart bypass surgery in Brazil was done at Portuguese Beneficent Hospital in São Paulo by Dr. Adib Jatene in 1968.

Baptist Church, where he had been a faithful member, and his body was buried at Vila Formosa Cemetery.

Daniel, with his family, went back to the State of Paraná to restart his life. He opened his own sales business, representing several companies from São Paulo in selling their products in that State. He did very well, paid all his debts and became a successful business man.

I continued my studies for the ministry. Paul wrote in his letter to the Galatians that he was chosen before he was born. "God in his grace chose me even before I was born, and called me to serve him" (Galatians 1:15 GNT). My mother once told me that, when I was to be born, she prayed to God and dedicated me to Him. This conversation with my Mom happened only a few years later when I was already in the ministry. I studied three years at the Brazilian Baptist School and five at the Baptist Seminary.

When Pastor Eneas Tognini left the Perdizes Baptist Church I stayed on as an assistant to Pastor Alberto Blanco de Oliveira, living in the same apartment at the back of the pastor's house. My main responsibility now was to travel every Sunday afternoon to the city of Atibaia, where our church was starting a new congregation. Every Sunday afternoon I led a group of young people from the church. On the main square of that city we conducted a service, talked to people and gave out leaflets. Sometimes during the week, I would travel to Atibaia to visit families who were interested in listening to the message of the gospel. I stayed as an assistant to Pastor Alberto Blanco de Oliveira for about one year, until I received an invitation from a small church in the city of Osasco and became the senior lead pastor, even though I was not yet ordained. I still had one more year to finish the Bachelor of Theology course at the Faculdade Teológica Batista.

9

&

A SPACIOUS BASEMENT APARTMENT

"It is smarter to plan ahead."
– Ecclesiastes 10:10b (GNT)

The São Paulo Faculdade Teológica Batista (Baptist Seminary) was founded on the first day of March 1957, in the building of the Brazilian Baptist School. Its first director was Dr. Lauro Bretones. Some years later the seminary moved to a large house at the corner of Homem de Melo Street and Ministro de Godoy Street, which in the past used to be the residence of the principal of the Brazilian Baptist School. The building had a large spacious apartment that was divided into several rooms to accommodate students who came from several cities to work and study in São Paulo. Some had a call to the ministry and were studying at the seminary. The price we had to pay to rent a room was very reasonable. Life was not easy in a big city like São Paulo.

When I moved from the state high school Col. Paulo Egídio de Oliveira Carvalho, in Vila Maria, to the Brazilian Baptist School to continue the Scientific Course, I was invited by Dr. Thurmon

Bryant to work in the office of the Baptist Seminary. My responsibility was to see that the students paid their fees and received all the information they needed. I worked in this position for some years. I knew of the difficult life of some of the students who lived at the school.

Colégio Batista Brasileiro (Brazilian Baptist School), São Paulo

Dona Maria was the caretaker of the house. Every day she prepared a delicious lunch for the students who arrived for the evening classes. One day, some of the students suggested that she also do dinner. She did it for some time, but she had to stop because she lived too far from the seminary and arrived home late and tired. So, talking to the students, who arrived tired for evening classes straight from their work, I volunteered to cook dinner for them, as I lived on the premises and had some spare time. They would pay for the groceries and I would get a free dinner! It was at this time that I perfected my culinary skills! Years later that dinner became what it is today – the canteen of the Faculdade Teológica Batista.

Sometime later, I went to visit the old house where the seminary used to be. I parked my car on Ministro de Godoy Street. I walked slowly until I came to the corner of Homem de Melo Street, where in those days there were a newspaper stand and a taxi stand. The students who lived in the spacious apartment were always the first to read the news of the day, the headlines that were recorded in history:

"Che Guevara Killed in Bolivia"
"John Lennon Says He Is More Popular than Jesus"
"João Goulart Leaves the Presidency"
"Santos Champion and Pelé Considered the King of Soccer"
"Corinthians Fails To Be Champion for Ten Years"

Dr. Thurmon Bryant, João Garcia, Prof. Paternostro and Deusdete Anselmo Duarte

The building was still there, clearly marked by time. I went up the short flight of stairs to the entrance door of the old house. Someone had left the door open. I entered and was compelled to go upstairs to the classrooms. However, at that moment the nostalgia took over and I turned to the right, still at the bottom of the stairs, and walked to the spacious basement apartment, which was now silent, taken by time, dark, full of cobwebs, cleaning forgotten, smelly and moldy.

Even so, I entered the spacious abandoned apartment and stayed standing there for a while remembering those long-gone days.

There, where there are no more rooms and the divisions are taken away, several young people lived some years of their lives dreaming about a great future. All of them came to the big city to work and study, without knowing we were making memories that would be in our minds forever. Where would all those students who lived there be? Not too long ago when Lucimar and I were staying at an apartment at Bombas Beach in Santa Catarina, Brazil, we received a visit from our wonderful friend, an ex-student at the seminary, Pastor Manoel Waldemur. He was brilliant. He studied theology at the seminary and philosophy at the Pontifícia Universidade Católica (PUC). After his studies he was ordained to the ministry, married and went to Joinville, Santa Catarina, where he and his wife opened a house to help orphan children. He did a great job helping dozens of children.

One day I was working at the seminary office when I heard a scream coming from the apartment. I went quickly to check what was happening. One of the students was crying with excruciating pain. Immediately I called a taxi and took him to a medical clinic. I waited until he was medicated, and we went back to the apartment. Sylvio Macri had come from Rio de Janeiro to study and work in São Paulo. He is now a pastor in Rio de Janeiro.

Some students at the seminary enjoyed playing and watching soccer. We agreed that it would be a good idea to go every Wednesday to the Pacaembu[29] Stadium, which was located not too far from the seminary, to watch a game. Sometimes we walked there after evening classes. Silas Costa sometimes took us in his car, always happy to do so. Many times, we saw Pelé and Garrincha playing, two famous Brazilian soccer players in the sixties. Those Wednesday nights were greatly anticipated!

Leaving the place, I turned and stopped for some time in front of the door that used to be the entrance to the office of the seminary, where I assisted all the students who came in with their questions. That door was now closed forever. The office is now in the new Faculdade Teológica Batista building, which is located across the corner from the Brazilian Baptist School at João Ramalho Street and Ministro de Godoy Street. I stayed standing there for a while, remembering the discussion I had with Dr. Thurmon Bryant about a book club that I wanted to start at the seminary. I had heard that, at

---

[29] *Wikipedia*, under the words "Pacaembu Stadium." A soccer stadium in the Pacaembu neighbourhood in São Paulo. It belongs to the city of São Paulo. It houses the Museu do Futebol, Brazil's national football museum.

the Southern Baptist Theological Seminary in Rio de Janeiro, they had started one which helped the students to buy books with great discounts straight from the printers. So, I wanted to start one at the seminary using the same model. He asked me to travel to Rio de Janeiro to get the information necessary to open a book club in our seminary. Professor Darci Dusileck, whom I knew, gave me all the instructions and together with the academic centre we started the book club. We bought books in Portuguese and English. Students paid a fee to become a member and bought books for a good discount.

I left that door of so many memories and walked up the steps that took the students to the classrooms. At the top of the stairs to the left there used to be the library where I spent some time studying. I walked to the chapel. I remembered when the great singer George Beverly Shea came to sing for the students. Billy Graham came twice to São Paulo to preach at the Pacaembu Stadium.

Every room in that old building was empty and very quiet. Now it is only the past that lives there! Memories! The Faculdade Teológica Batista has been moved to the new building. It is a great school and continues to prepare students for the ministry.

That spacious apartment taught us many lessons. We learned the great value of living in community. We were young and preparing for the same goal. We looked with hope to future ministry. We still didn't know where God would take us. Each one of us had the conviction that we were not alone, that we came together to that seminary because God had brought us there. We learned about human nature and our weaknesses, anxieties and problems. We understood that without love, patience, persistence and prayer it was impossible to be in the pastoral ministry, to which God had called us. I always thank God for having lived in that apartment with the other students. It will always be in my memory.

10

&

CAN I HELP?

*"God always provides another person
to whom we can show our love."
– João Garcia*

In my last year at the São Paulo Faculdade Teológica Batista, I felt like leaving Perdizes Baptist Church, where I had been an assistant to the senior pastor, and looking for a church that would take me as a part-time minister, although I had not been ordained as I was still a student. When the professors and students heard that I was prepared to take such a position, an invitation soon came from Bela Vista Baptist Church, a small church in Osasco, a small satellite town on the periphery of São Paulo. I accepted the invitation, moved my membership and every weekend travelled to Osasco. I preached in the church on Sundays at morning and evening services. I also led the youth meetings and visited in the area where the church was located. It was a lot of work on the weekends, but I never complained. Bela Vista was a church with many possibilities, and I was glad I could help.

It was there that I met a beautiful and wonderful young lady, Lucimar Calvello. She was from Avaré, a city in the South of the State of São Paulo. Her mother was a descendant of German and Spanish families and her father of an Italian family. She was a member of Avaré Baptist Church. When she finished her elementary teacher training, she decided to go to university to study psychology. So, she moved to São Paulo to prepare for the entrance examination. She was living in a hostel not too far from where I lived at the Baptist Seminary. To pay for her expenses she found a job at the Itaú Bank and went to the preparatory school in the evening. One Sunday morning she came to my church with a couple of church members who were friends of her family. After the service I greeted them and invited them to come next week for a conference.

That week in March 1968, we were going to have an evangelistic conference. The guest speaker was Rev. Alberto Blanco. I asked Lucimar whether she was interested in coming. "Would you like to come to the conference?"

"I need transportation."

"I think that Alberto Blanco wouldn't mind if you come with me in his car. He is going to take me."

I didn't have a car and neither did she. She was studying and so was I. I was in my last year at the Faculdade Teológica Batista. She wanted to be a psychologist. She never thought that her life was about to change to be that of a pastor's wife. Once, she had told herself that she would never be a pastor's wife!

I asked Alberto Blanco whether he could take Lucimar too in his car.

"It would be a pleasure," he answered.

Every night of the conference I would go to pick her up, by bus as far as Rev. Alberto Blanco's house, and from there we would go in his car to Osasco, where the church was located. Saturday, we got there a little early. We noticed that the church had been used for a wedding. The sanctuary was a mess. The chairs had been put in one corner and rice was everywhere on the floor. In the Brazilian culture it is customary to throw rice at the newly married couple for luck! Imagine this in a Baptist church! The newly married couple had left, the invited guests as well, and no one was in charge of cleaning or arranging the sanctuary for the conference that would follow.

I looked at the clock on the wall; time was flying! Soon the service had to start, and I was concerned. So, I got a broom and began to sweep the floor. Lucimar watched me sweeping and she asked me politely whether she could help. "Can I help you?"

How could I reject such a polite offer! "Of course," I answered gratefully.

I gave her the broom and moved on to another job, putting the chairs back where they belonged. It was that day that I felt God was showing me my future wife.

Sunday evening, after the service, I took her home, but not by car. We took the bus, then the train to Sorocabana Station and another bus to where she lived in Santa Cecília. Before I took her to her house we went to a small restaurant and that night I asked her whether she would be my girlfriend.

I had left my heart in Mandaguaçu (Big Bee), but I found a new one in Avaré, São Paulo. With this new love, a new life began. God was guiding me, and also her. Now Lucimar did not have to prepare herself to be a psychologist, but she could think about being a pastor's wife. This would be God's plan for us, but not just by chance.

In her book, *The Hiding Place,* Corrie ten Boom[30] writes about the history of her family who helped many Jews from Amsterdam, Holland, to escape from the Nazi persecution. Corrie had a sister called Betsie who, when she faced many difficulties, always said that she had to give thanks to God. She went through a very sad experience in her own life; her boyfriend had left her and she was suffering a lot. One day she was sad and crying. Her father came to comfort her and said that God always provides another opportunity, another person to whom we can show our love. I believe that God provided me with the other person to whom I could show all my love. Lucimar became the love of my life. I finished my B.Th. degree in November 1968. It took me five years doing the Scientific Course and another five years to

---

[30] I heard Corrie ten Boom speak at the Presbyterian Cathedral in São Paulo and in London, England. I read her book, *The Hiding Place,* in English and Portuguese. She was an amazing Christian Dutch woman who was in Ravensbruk concentration camp during the Second World War. (See the article by Dr. James Emery White, "The Ten Boom House: Trusting God's Will," at https://www.crosswalk.com/blogs/dr-james-emery-white/the-ten-boom-house-trusting-gods-will.html .)

finish the B.Th. at the Faculdade Teológica Batista – ten years of studies in São Paulo.

I always thought of continuing to study, even after becoming a pastor. In August of 1968, I had a wonderful surprise, that I considered to be the hand of God in my life. He is always with us; we never walk alone. He opens doors when we want to serve Him. The apostle Peter said in his first letter that as Christians we should "leave all your worries with him, because he cares for you" (1 Peter 5:7).

11

ABBEY ROAD, LONDON, ENGLAND, 1969

"Give yourself to the LORD; *trust in him, and he will help you"*
– Psalm 37:5

     In the summer of 1968, I had a visit from a missionary couple, whom I knew well, at the São Paulo Faculdade Teológica Batista. They worked with the Baptist Missionary Society of London, England, (BMS) in the city of Umuarama, State of Paraná, Brazil. On my holidays I used to visit my brother and his family, who lived in that city. On one of those visits I met Pastor David and Doris Doonan. They were my brother's neighbours, and we became friends and often had conversations about São Paulo, churches, my studies and my future ministry.

     When they came to visit me, David asked, "João, are you planning to continue studying when you finish your degree at the São Paulo Faculdade Teológica Batista?"

     "Yes," I answered him, "I am in my last year of my Bachelor Degree."

David then told me the history of Spurgeon's College, in London, England. Charles Haddon Spurgeon[31] was a great evangelical Baptist preacher. His conversion happened on January 6, 1850, when he was 15 years old, in the city of Colchester, in southeast England. That Sunday he was on his way to a meeting. It was winter and very cold; snow started to fall, and the wind was strong. Suddenly it became a storm! Spurgeon, then, took shelter in a Primitive Methodist Chapel. The service was starting, but the pastor was absent, because of the storm. A layman, possibly a shoemaker or a tailor, a simple man, preached the message based on the verse Isaiah 45:22. The prophet was asking people to turn to God to be saved. At the end of the sermon the preacher, looking at Spurgeon, made an appeal in a loud voice, "Young man, look to Jesus Christ and be saved." God opened Charles's heart that night and he was saved.

On May 3rd of the same year he was baptized by immersion in the River Lark, in Isleham, a small village in Cambridgeshire in East Anglia, England. Even without having had theological studies, he started preaching at 16 years of age. At 19 he was invited to be the pastor of a large church, New Park Street Chapel, Southwark, a subdivision of London.

Some years later he moved to Metropolitan Tabernacle, at the Elephant and Castle junction, south of London. The Tabernacle in those days was the largest Baptist church in the world. He was the pastor there for thirty-eight years, preaching to an average of five thousand people every Sunday. Many were converted, and several churches founded in London. He was known as the "Prince of Preachers," the best preacher during the time of Queen Victoria.[32] His sermons are still read and translated into many languages. One of his goals in the ministry was to teach young people to preach. In 1857 he started, at the Tabernacle, a school for young people who were called to the ministry. In the beginning the school was called the Pastor's

---

[31] Founder of Spurgeon's College with the purpose of preparing young men for the ministry. See the book, *Spurgeon*, The Banner of Truth Trust, 1861. (I have a copy in my library.)

[32] *Wikipedia*, under the words Charles Spurgeon, "7 October 1857, he preached to the largest crowd ever – 23,654 people – at The Crystal Palace in London.

College, later was renamed to Spurgeon's College, and was moved to the present building, on South Norwood Hill, South London.

David told me, "There is a possibility of getting a scholarship for you to study at Spurgeon's College." And he continued, "If you want, I can present your name to the principal, Dr. Beasley-Murray."

I answered that it was important to me to pursue higher education. I had always wanted to continue studying before being ordained. I would be very happy if he introduced me to Dr. Beasley-Murray. It would entail so many things and changes in my life, if I were accepted. I then invited Pastor David and Mrs. Doris Doonan for dinner at my mother's home in Vila Alpina, São Paulo. During and after dinner we continued talking about my possible move to London, England, to study at Spurgeon's College.

The next day they travelled to England. A few days after their arrival in London, Pastor David visited the college for a meeting with Dr. Beasley-Murray, to introduce me as a possible candidate for a scholarship that was available for a foreigner student.

A few weeks later I received a letter from Dr. Beasley-Murray saying that the college had considered the presentation of Pastor David Doonan and was very happy to accept me as a student for the B.D. program starting in September 1969.

However, this offer was conditional on my passing a test that I would be given in English for reading, writing and speaking fluently, plus a test in New Testament Koine Greek. I had to pass both tests! With the letter, he also sent me a New Testament Greek grammar, *The Elements of New Testament Greek*, by J. W. Wenham, Vice-Principal of Tyndale Hall, Bristol. I had to know that grammar by heart before entering the college! This was August 1968, and by September 1969 I had to be ready to take both tests and pass!

I answered immediately, accepting the challenge. I had studied English at a school in downtown São Paulo, but it was not sufficient, and I had also studied Greek at the Baptist Seminary. I had some knowledge of it, but not sufficient to take a test. So, I would have a lot of studies ahead of me before September 1969.

I started to look for a school of English in London, England, that could accept me as a student and give me some work to pay for my studies. I wrote a letter to the Brazilian Consulate in London, to the Brazilian Chamber of Commerce and also to a friend whom I knew in Rio de Janeiro at Copacabana Baptist Church. Waldemiro

Tymchak had finished his Bachelor of Theology at the Baptist Seminary in Rio and had gone to Spurgeon's College with the same type of scholarship I was about to receive. He was there in his second year. I explained to him that I needed to know English well before entering college and was looking for a language school in London that could take me as a student and also employ me so that I could pay for my studies.

Waldemiro wrote back saying that he knew a Christian school in London that taught English to students that came from different countries. Most of these students were missionaries who needed English in order to do their missionary work in the countries where they were going to serve. The school employed some of the students to pay for their tuition. He sent me the address of the Abbey Christian School for the English Language at 16a Abbey Road, in front of EMI Studios, where the Beatles were recording their songs. I was so grateful to Waldemiro and immediately wrote to the school's principal explaining my situation.

The school was located at the Abbey Road Baptist Church. It was an old church building that in the past had had a very large congregation, with 750 pews all numbered, but in the sixties was very small, almost empty. In 1962 Rev. L. R. Barnard, the pastor, started the Abbey Christian School for the English Language for missionaries who needed English to do their ministries, as most students came from the Continent.

The reply I received from the school was signed by the principal, Miss Valerie Lawrence, and mentioned, among other things, that, if I accepted their offer to be a student at the school, I was expected to work five hours a day. I had to arrive in London no later than January 10, 1969. As payment they would offer room and board, tuition for five hours a day and two pounds sterling weekly. I answered immediately, accepting the offer, and started preparing myself for the trip to London.

I had enough savings to buy my ticket and some extras that I could take with me for my first days in London. I went to Varig, the Brazilian airlines, and bought my ticket. A few weeks later I received a letter from the school, which I had to present to the British Consulate, located on Paulista Avenue, São Paulo, with my request for a visa. It didn't take too long before I received the student visa; I was ready to travel.

Call and Preparation

Abbey Road Baptist Church,
where the English language school was located

I explained to my family that everything was in order for my trip. My mother was somewhat surprised and asked me why I had to go so far to continue studying! I answered her that God was in it and that He had a purpose for my life. She accepted it and said she would be praying for me.

Saturday afternoon, I went to see Lucimar. As we ate pizza in our favourite pizzeria, I explained to her in detail what was going on regarding my studies in London. "I received a letter from Spurgeon's College," I said.

"What is the answer?" she asked.

"I was accepted; I will start in September 1969," and I continued, telling her that I had found a school in London where I could work and study English, before I started college in the fall.

She was very sad! I promised her that I was going, but I would come back to her. The following week I went with her to Avaré,[33] where her parents lived, and explained everything to them. Our time in São Paulo was wonderful. We were always together. Every Saturday I would go to meet her, together we went to the youth meeting and on Sundays we would go to the morning and evening services. Sometimes, when I had a free weekend, we would go to the beaches in Santos. We also visited my mother's home in Parque São Lucas.

The day of my departure for London arrived. I arranged my suitcases at Euclides and Tatá's house[34], and took them to the veranda. I made sure I had the passport and ticket in my hand; before leaving we prayed together. A lot of emotions! All my sisters, my brother-in-law, my Mom and Lucimar went to the airport with me. We took two taxis to accommodate all of us. We had to go through the terrible São Paulo traffic, and we arrived at the Congonhas Airport, which at that time was the only airport in São Paulo. It was very busy with lots of people travelling to different parts of the world. For me it was like a dream! I had never thought that I would study in London, England.

I took my luggage to the Varig check-in; I waited in the line-up for a while, took my luggage to be weighed and showed my documents, including the letter from Abbey Christian School for the English Language that showed I was registered as a student at the school and another letter from Spurgeon's College.

The young lady who helped me at Varig's wicket was very polite, checked all my documents – everything was in order – dispatched the luggage and said, "Have a good trip," giving me the boarding pass. The trip would be from São Paulo to Rio, Lisbon, Paris and London, in a Boeing 707, on January 9, 1969.

We stayed a little longer talking with each other. When I had to say goodbye some more tears came! I hugged everyone, put my hand baggage on the belt for inspection by federal police and moved out of sight. I waited in the Varig hall until my flight was called. All

---

[33] A city three hundred kilometres south of São Paulo
[34] My sister Carmen and her husband Euclides. We always called her Tatá, because she was very kind and close to all her brothers and sisters. She was like a nanny to all of us.

we passengers embarked on a Boeing 707, destination London, England.

There was a mixture of happiness and apprehension about the future. Many questions filled my mind. How would my life be in London? Would I be successful? Could I learn English and know my Greek grammar before entering college? What about my family and Lucimar? God was giving me a great opportunity and I had to trust that He was present in my life and guiding my paths.

Soon after all passengers were accommodated, the pilot announced the take-off of the Boeing 707 destined for London, England, with stops in Rio, Lisbon and Paris. It was a long trip from Rio to Lisbon. A dinner was served. After that I took my New Testament from my pocket to read. The passenger beside me saw it, was very surprised that I was reading the New Testament and started a conversation. "Are you going to Paris?" he asked me.

"No, I am going to London," I answered.

And he continued, asking what I was going to do in London.

"I am going to study theology," I answered him.

He was even more surprised that a young man like me would go to London to study theology! The sixties were years of the Beatles, hippies, revolution and great demonstrations in Chicago and Paris. Maybe he thought that I was involved in one of these movements in Europe. I really didn't know what he was thinking.

He continued the conversation, saying, "I work for Air France; I am going back to Paris," and then he said, "I don't believe in God."

I had to say to him that I was there beside him, travelling to London, because God had brought me to that moment in time, and that He was guiding my paths. I never walked alone; He was always with me.

The young man stared at me probably thinking that I was an extra-terrestrial! I then remembered the words written by the prophet Isaiah a long time ago, "… those who wait for the LORD shall renew their strength, they shall mount up with wings like eagles, they shall run and not be weary, they shall walk and not faint" (Isaiah 40:31). I was flying very high, not only physically, but spiritually!

The conversation stopped at that point. I slept. I woke up with the announcement that we were landing shortly at Portela Airport in Lisbon. All passengers had to leave the aircraft and wait in the airport terminal until we were called to continue the flight to Paris, where again we had to get off and wait until we continued the last part of the flight, which was to London. We arrived late afternoon. I had two small bags; I put them on an airport cart, and pushed it into the Heathrow Airport. The officer looked at me and took my documents, my passport, the letter from Abbey Christian School and another from Spurgeon's College. Then, looking at me again, he asked with a strong Londoner accent, "Do you bring spirits?"

I didn't understand what he meant. I couldn't answer!

He asked again, "Do you bring spirits?"

As I couldn't answer him because I did not understand his question, he told me to go with my luggage to another table. I went to the table he pointed out, where another officer was checking passengers' luggage. I stood in line until my turn came. I approached the table, I put my luggage on it and the officer asked me the same question, "Do you bring spirits?" Again, I couldn't answer. Then he asked me to open my luggage. I opened it. The first thing he saw was my Bible on top of my clothes. Then, immediately, he said that I could close it and go. So, probably he guessed that I was a Christian and, of course, did not bring any spirits into the country!

I walked very slowly, pushing my luggage, a little bit confused, taking my Bible under my arm, as I did not put it back in the luggage. I was now in the large hall of the Heathrow Airport – so many people around me, coming and going – when I saw at a distance two men waving to me. They were my friends Waldemiro Tymchak and Pastor David Doonan. A great relief! A huge weight was lifted off me! I walked faster, I came out and they welcomed me to London, England. "Welcome, welcome, *bem-vindo*, to London," they said.

I was so happy to meet them. Coming from a small countryside pioneer town in the State of Paraná, Brazil, it was like a dream to arrive in London and be welcomed by wonderful friends.

Waldemiro then asked me whether I just arrived from Brazil ready to evangelize England. I didn't know what he meant, but he was referring to the Bible I had under my arm.

"No," I answered, "I came to study!"

"And the Bible under your arm?" he asked.

"Well, the officer asked me whether I had brought 'spirits'. As I didn't know what 'spirits' is, he asked me to open my luggage to check. When he saw my Bible on top of my clothes, he said I was okay and could go, and I forgot to put my Bible back inside the luggage." Speaking in Portuguese, I asked my friends the translation for 'spirits'.

They both answered at the same time, *"Bebidas alcoólicas, alcoholic drinks."*

I was so surprised because in my mind I was thinking, "How come he knows I am a Christian, asking me about the 'Spirit'?" We had a good laugh!

It was a Friday night, January 10, 1969. Pastor David and Waldemiro took me to Spurgeon's College, in the south of London, where Dr. Beasley-Murray received me on behalf of the college. Together we had a light lunch in the dining hall; after that David left and Waldmiro, who was a student at the college, took me to the guest room. That night I slept deeply.

Saturday morning's sunrise was beautiful, even though it was winter. After breakfast, Miss Pam Neville, the nutritionist of the college, took Waldemiro and me to the language school, in St. John's Wood, an elegant Jewish quarter of London. It was on the other side of the city, and we had to go through downtown. For the first time I saw the Thames River, the Houses of Parliament, Westminster Abbey, Trafalgar Square, Piccadilly Circus and finally Abbey Road. We passed in front of EMI Studios, where the Beatles used to record their music and where they were photographed crossing the famous pedestrian zebra, which became the cover of their album *Abbey Road*.

I got out of the car, took my luggage, entered the school hall, waited until the principal, Miss Valerie Lawrence, came and Pam Neville and Waldemiro introduced me to her. We went to the sitting room and had a cup of tea and a conversation of which I didn't understand a word. Then Waldemiro and Pam took me to my room and went back to the college. Miss Lawrence went to her office. I stayed alone in my room opening my luggage and putting things in the closet and then, very tired, I had a nap. There, in that small room of Abbey Christian School, I began thinking and praying about the next days at the school. From Monday, January 12, 1969, I would have several responsibilities. There would be my School for the English Language and work, before I went to Spurgeon's College in September.

After a while, I woke up and I had to go to the washroom. The problem was that I didn't know how to say washroom in English – *banheiro* in Portuguese. I went out of my room, looking for the washroom. I opened several doors, but I couldn't find it. Then I tried to talk to an English teacher who was playing snooker with a student from Finland. The snooker table was located in the entrance hall. I tried to explain my need, but nobody understood what I wanted. Then, the student might have guessed it, and said to the teacher something like this: "I think I know what he needs."

I didn't understand what he said, but I followed him, and he took me to the "toilet." That is the proper English word in England for washroom. I never forgot it – "toilet."

I continued tidying up my room. I was happy. Later that afternoon someone knocked at the door. I opened it; a middle-aged gentleman, smiling and talking in Portuguese with an accent, asked me, "Are you João Garcia, the new student from Brazil?"

I answered, "*Sim, Senhor*! (Yes, Sir!)"

"Welcome to London," and he continued, speaking in Portuguese, "I am the pastor of the church; my name is Clifford Parsons." He told me that he had been a missionary in Angola, Africa, for twenty-five years. When he finished his work in Africa he came back to London and accepted the invitation of Abbey Road Baptist Church to be the pastor. As the school was located by the church building, he was also an English teacher.

Then he invited me for a walk. "João, would you like to go for a walk to Regent's Park?" I understood because he spoke in Portuguese.

We walked to Regent's Park and to Primrose Hill and then we went back to Abbey Road. Pastor Clifford and I were talking about Brazil, Angola and my future time at Surgeon's College. He told me about his missionary work in Cabinda, Angola, a very important area of the country. Cabinda is where petroleum was found. During the revolution in the Angolan War of Independence from Portugal (1961-1974) different groups like the MPLA, FNLA and UNITA were interested in capturing Cabinda. Clifford was a socialist and always defending the poor. The government, still in power at this time in Cabinda, was Portuguese, and he was expelled from the country, considered *persona non grata*. So, Clifford and Lottie had to go back to England. They became our great Christian friends in England and more than friends; they were like our parents in London.

Abbey Road, London, England, where the Beatles crossed
In the background, EMI Studios, where they recorded

Abbey Road became very famous all over the world because of the Beatles. They recorded at EMI Studios. In 1969 they were at the top of their success. The young people knew when they were going to be at EMI Studios and gathered in front of it. Hundreds of them awaited their arrival for hours. A few times I had to go through the crowd when walking to the Underground station. When Lucimar came to study at the school we sometimes sat on a bench on the corner in front of EMI Studios and talked about our future. She was studying for the Lower and Proficiency Cambridge English examinations. These would give her both certificates from Cambridge University for foreign students. She could use these qualifications to teach English in Brazil. I was at Spurgeon's College and I could teach at a seminary and be a pastor in a local church. On our return to Brazil we did exactly this in Curitiba, Paraná.

On my first Sunday at school Waldemiro invited me to go for a walk in downtown London. First, we went to the 6 p.m. service at All Souls Anglican Church, where the pastor was the famous Rev.

John Stott.[35] After the service we walked to Piccadilly Circus, talking about college and life in general in England, especially about the situation of the Baptist churches. I had to be very well prepared psychologically and spiritually. It would be a long walk always obeying the call of God.

There were many, many people at Piccadilly Circus – a lot of hippies sitting on the ground, smoking and some playing guitar. About ten o'clock we went to the Piccadilly Underground station. Waldemiro went back to the College and I went to the School. Both of us took the Waterloo Line, he to Elephant and Castle and I to St. John's Wood Station. That night I got my first impression of London, a city of immigrants and tourists. In Piccadilly you could hear people speaking all different languages except English, the language of Shakespeare! It sounded like a Tower of Babel.

Every Sunday afternoon the school had a meeting for young people called "International at Home." Students from the school and also some from London University, came to the meeting, which was led by Rev. Clifford Parsons. Every Sunday a subject was discussed. At the first meeting every student was introduced, and each had to say his or her name, his nationality and what he was doing in London. When my turn came, because I did not speak good English yet, Rev. Parsons introduced me saying that I was from Brazil and then he asked me in Portuguese what I was doing in London. I promptly answered, thinking that I knew English, "I pretend to study at Spurgeon's College."

Everybody laughed! I did not know why. What happened was that the word *pretender* in Portuguese means "to intend." In my mind I was saying "pretend," meaning that I was going to study at Spurgeon's College. But the students were understanding that I was going to "fake" study. Rev. Clifford Parsons, who spoke Portuguese, knew exactly what was going on in my mind and explained to the students the difference between "to pretend" in English and *"pretender"* in Portuguese. I was a little embarrassed by the mistake! I had a long way to go to learn the English language.

---

[35] Rev. John Stott was a famous evangelical Anglican preacher, who was known all over the world and who wrote several books. He died July 27, 2011.

Call and Preparation

After the meeting, Waldemiro and I walked through Oxford Street, Leicester Square, Soho and Trafalgar Square. I was amazed that I was walking on these streets of London, England. Up to the age of sixteen I lived in a small village far away in Brazil, Mandaguaçu (Big Bee). I also understood with gratitude that it was God Who brought me, at that time, to study at the most prestigious Baptist college in England, linked to the University of London. It was marvelous; what a blessing!

One day the following week I decided to go out alone for the first time to discover London. With a guide in my hands I went around the new and old downtown. I walked along many streets. Each street, each corner and every stone told some of the history of London. I could come very close to the site that was destroyed by the great fire September 2 to 5, 1666.[36] Sadly I saw the places that were bombed by Nazi airplanes. Tired of walking I sat down at Piccadilly Circus and observed the great number of hippies, some sleeping, although it was a sunny day, some playing guitars and others just talking and laughing. Some of these young men left their homes looking for a free life, away from the discipline of their parents. I came back to Piccadilly Circus many times. Sometimes I sat with them too. It was quite interesting to talk to them. One day I went with a group of Christian young people. We sat beside them, sang gospel songs and talked about Jesus, as much as they would listen. On one of those visits a young lady showed interest and wanted to come with us to the school. We were very happy to take her with us for a visit. She liked it so much that she asked the principal, Miss Valerie Lawrence, whether she could stay, living there. She was accepted and stayed working at the school.

This young lady was an American from California; she was married and travelled with her husband to India; there they separated, and she came to London. She went to Piccadilly Circus and joined the group of hippies that had taken over the square. I talked to her several times and she always had a story about her life. One day she told me how much she wanted to see her parents again and tell them what had

---

[36] *Wikipedia*, under the words "Great Fire of London." 13,200 houses and 87 churches were destroyed, and unknown numbers of people died.

happened in her life. Listening to the gospel at the school she accepted Jesus, she was baptized and her life was transformed to the point of becoming a wonderful witness for Jesus Christ. When we went back to Brazil she was still living at the school.

Three months after my arrival at the school I was already speaking English enough to understand and be understood. It was very difficult to work and study, but by the grace of God I did it. My scholarship at Spurgeon's College was conditional on passing tests that I had to take in English and Koine Greek, the language in which the New Testament was written.

At the English school I met several students from the Continent. A couple and their two children, from Finland, were going as missionaries to Ceylon. I also had a very good friend who was a girl from Finland, Ulla Sepala. Peter Schaub, my roommate, from Switzerland, needed the English language because he was going to work with the Red Cross. A young lady from Germany was called to the ministry. She applied to the Irish Baptist College, affiliated with Queen's University, Belfast, and was accepted. She left the school and went to Northern Ireland. John Neale was a teacher at the school. He became a good friend. We enjoyed talking about theology. Brian was an excellent organist. He was very quiet, but I managed to get him to speak a little bit. Where would all of them be now?

The school promoted outings to different places of interest to the students. I always took advantage of those trips. When Lucimar arrived at the school we always used to go together when we were available. We visited Stratford-upon-Avon, where Shakespeare was born and lived. He is buried at Holy Trinity Church, in the same city. We visited the historic Canterbury Cathedral, the seat of the Archbishop of Canterbury, leader of the Church of England. We visited, several times, the Universities of Cambridge and Oxford, two of the most important in the world. In London we visited the Houses of Parliament and Westminster Cathedral, where, in the centre of the nave, is buried David Livingstone, the great physician, explorer and missionary in Africa.

Almost every evening, after dinner, I would go to the St. John's Wood Library, located at Finchley Road, to study my Koine Greek grammar, that Dr. Beasley-Murray had sent me when I was still at the Faculdade Teológica Batista in São Paulo. I had to know that grammar by heart in order to take the test the first week of September

1969. I was one of the fifteen students who had to take the test and passed with a good mark. I was the only foreigner! This encouraged me for the studies that were about to begin.

In June the school closed for the summer. Students went back to their countries, but I had to stay until September. The building was almost empty. I had an idea. I didn't want to stay in the building doing nothing for three months! So, I spoke to the principal, Valerie Lawrence. "Miss Lawrence, I would prefer to find work outside the school, and, if I find a job, I could pay my expenses."

She thought it was an excellent idea. She accepted my suggestion and I started looking for a job. As I had lived ten years in a big city like São Paulo, I knew that there were many jobs in London. It was a question of looking for one. Every day I read the advertisement page of some London papers that I bought at the newsstand.

One day, however, I met a pastor who knew I was going to study at Spurgeon's College. He had studied there too and knew Waldemiro, my Brazilian friend. He informed me that the Inner London Education Authority[37] was looking for students who could work part-time to do some jobs in schools. I went immediately to speak to Mr. Sengupta, who was the person responsible for the Department of Human Resources. He interviewed me and with a wonderful smile he asked, "Would you like to start immediately?"

"Yes, of course," I answered.

He gave me a note and said, "Go, then, to the principal of Trinity School at Elephant and Castle, give her this note and say that I sent you."

It was a girls' school. There I worked until the end of August. I lived at Abbey Christian School, but I worked at Trinity School over the summer. In time my English became much better.

---

[37] Established in 1965 to foster education in the City of London

12

SPURGEON'S COLLEGE

"Et Teneo, Et Teneor"
(I hold and I am held)
– Spurgeon's College motto

On September 27, 1969, I entered Spurgeon's College, South Norwood Hill, London, England, a large Victorian building. Waldemiro Tymchak was a student at the college. It was wonderful to have a friend from Brazil and be able to speak Portuguese once in a while! He was a great friend. We were always together talking about our future back in Brazil. In 1970 he was invited to visit Russia to preach. He had been born in Brazil, but his parents were from Bessarabia, Romania.[38] At the college there were, for a short while, two students from Russia, and they arranged Waldemiro's visit with all expenses paid by the Russian Baptists. He preached in several churches and a few times at the First Baptist Church in Moscow. He was very emotional about visiting Russia!

---

[38]Today Bessarabia is called Maldovia. In 1940 Russia took over the region and many Bessarabians emigrated to Brazil.

When he came back, he wrote several articles for the Brazilian Baptist newspaper *O Jornal Batista* that I had the privilege to read and type before they were sent to be published. Waldemiro asked me to type them, which I did using the Abbey Christian School office typewriter. *O Jornal Batista* published seven articles. Thousands of people were moved emotionally after reading those articles. He titled them "I Cried in Russia."

As soon as he finished his studies at Spurgeon's College, he went back to Brazil to teach at the Baptist Theological Seminary of Paraná in Curitiba. He also became a pastor at a small Baptist church in Pilarzinho, a subdivision of Curitiba. Two years later I followed him at the same institution, where I taught New Testament theology. After a few years in Curitiba he was invited to be the Executive Secretary of the World Mission Board of the Brazilian Baptist Convention, whose office is located in Rio de Janeiro.

Spurgeon's College on South Norwood Hill, SE London, England

For three years I studied full time at the College, enrolled in the Bachelor of Divinity course. To live full time at a college in England was a great blessing in my life. It was a very disciplined life – 7 a.m. breakfast, then prayers at the chapel, followed by lectures until 12 noon and then lunch. After lunch, there were students' meetings every day. From 2 p.m. to 4 p.m. was free time. At 4 p.m.

every student was in his room with a closed door and studying until 10 p.m. with a short break for supper and prayers at the chapel. After 10 p.m. there was a break for tea with friends, followed by sleeping in absolute silence, sometimes broken by the steps of a student walking in the direction of the phone booth, which was not allowed!

We studied in our rooms and in the library for research. My readings and studies were in New Testament theology; for this I had to study Greek, grammar and reading. As my English was not yet one hundred per cent, my English grammar book was always beside me. To study was a pleasure; so, I did not spend time on other things. It was a very profitable time and I felt very privileged to study at such a prestigious college.

Our college class, 1969

One of my tutors, Dr. Beasley-Murray, a great man of God, was Principal of Spurgeon's College. He was Professor of New Testament and Exegesis. He wrote several books; one of them is a classic study on Christian baptism, *Baptism in the New Testament*[39], which was

---

[39] G. R. Beasley-Murray, *Baptism in the New Testament*, Wm. B. Eerdmans Publishing Co., 1973.

translated into several languages. He guided me to study the theology of Dr. Oscar Cullmannn, a Lutheran theologian and a New Testament scholar at the University of Basel, Switzerland, and Sorbonne University in Paris. Dr. Cullmann wrote The *Christology of the New Testament* and also *Christ and Time: The Primitive Christian Conception of Time and History*. Dr. Beasley-Murray encouraged me to write several essays about what Cullmann had written on the primitive conception of time and history. Cullmann wrote that salvation history is a continuous time process in the past, present and future, that takes place in an ascending time line that has a beginning and an end, different from secular history that has a beginning, climax and then a decline. The centre of salvation history is the redemption by Christ on the cross and His resurrection.

Dr. Billy Graham visited London, England, in 1970. He had several meetings with pastors and leaders of evangelical churches. He also visited Spurgeon's College, spoke to the students and gave an invitation to some students for a breakfast at Grosvenor House, Park Lane. I was one of the students who received an invitation. I was very happy indeed for such an honour as to eat breakfast with Billy Graham. In 1962 he preached in São Paulo at the soccer stadium, Pacaembu Stadium. I had the privilege of being one of many who helped to organize the Billy Graham evangelistic campaign. I also heard him preaching at the Maracanã soccer stadium to 200,000 people at the conclusion of the World Baptist Alliance congress in 1960 in Rio.

The College closed for two weeks for Christmas holidays. I needed to find a job to earn some money. Lucimar was coming at the end of December. Once again, I was employed by the Inner London Education Authority. I was given a job for two weeks at a school in the south of London. I started at 6 a.m. and worked until 10 p.m. My responsibility was to keep the furnace fed with coal to have the school warm even during Christmas holidays. I had the wonderful opportunity to pray and study, especially my Greek grammar!

13

&

LOVE LETTERS FROM HERE AND THERE

"Memory always takes us to love letters."
– Anonymous

When I left São Paulo to go to England, Lucimar went back to her parents' home in Avaré, a small city in the State of São Paulo. She got a job in a factory office. We wrote letters to each other, from here and there. In the letters I always told her that I was talking to the principal of Abbey Christian School about the possibility of her coming to work and study at the school.

It didn't take too long, and Miss Valerie Lawrence gave me the good news that there was an opening for Lucimar to study and work at the school. I sent her the information and she discussed it with her parents, who agreed that she could go to London. Lucimar then started the process, providing her documents to the British Consulate in São Paulo and getting her passport and student visa. She bought her airline ticket at Varig Airlines, and travelled to London, via Lisbon and Paris, December 20, 1970. Finally, Lucimar would arrive!

On that day I went to the Heathrow Airport in London to wait for her arrival. It had rained a lot in Paris and the flight was delayed. I had to wait, according to the information I received. Finally, about 5 p.m., she arrived. She was very tired! It was a wonderful time! It had been one year since we had seen each other. I took her luggage, and we walked to the Underground and took the tube to Abbey Christian School. When we arrived Mr. and Mrs. Parsons were waiting for us with a delicious English supper. They were very surprised at how young Lucimar was, coming from so far away to work and study. Nothing was easy for us those days! It was a great challenge she had in front of her.

The school not only taught English, but prepared students who were interested in courses at Cambridge University. First, they had to take the basic Lower Cambridge Examination and upon approval they would take the Proficiency Course, which included English literature. Lucimar spent hours studying and working. She was successful and was approved in both courses and received her certificates.[40]

The beginning of her life in London was very stressful. We had been separated from each other for one year. Besides, I was in Spurgeon's College, in the south of London, and she was at Abbey School, in the north of London. Everything had changed and we had to face the situation. We needed to re-adapt ourselves to each other and this caused several difficulties. Pastor Clifford and Lottie Parsons were like parents to us, and God was in control.

Lucimar's cousin Sylvia, a very good companion for Lucimar, came the following year to Abbey School to work and study English. She met another student, from Switzerland, Peter Eglin, and after they finished their studies they were married in Brazil; now they live in Basel, Switzerland. I had the privilege of marrying them at the Avaré Baptist Church, in the summer of 1973.

Lucimar and I decided that we should be officially engaged. We followed the Brazilian tradition; as we did not have any family in

---

[40] Certificates of Lucimar Calvello: University of Cambridge, Local Examination Syndicate, Lower Certificate in English, Certificate of Proficiency in English. The examination is approved by the Department of Education and Science of Her Britannic Majesty's Government, December 1971, Index number 8901 047, Place of Examination London.

England, we invited our friend Waldemiro Tymchak, and on a Saturday evening we went to the college chapel and there I gave Lucimar her engagement ring. Waldemiro read the Bible and shared some thoughts and we three prayed together. After that we went to an Italian restaurant at Leicester Square to celebrate with a delicious dinner, thinking about our family in Brazil.

We were very happy although life was not easy those days. But we were determined to study as much as we could to go back to Brazil well prepared. I was allowed to go out of the College only on weekends. If I needed or wanted to go out before then, I had to get permission from the principal. He checked everyone and would approve or not. Every student had his own room where he slept and studied. For three years that was my home.

At the beginning of my second year in college I was taken ill with some stomach problems and went to the emergency department of St. Mary's Hospital in Paddington, in the west of London. I was hospitalized for special treatment. This hospital is part of the federal University of London. In the second week of my stay, a professor of medicine brought several students to my room. He was teaching the students how to diagnose a patient. When he looked at my eyes, he noticed that there was a scar in my right eye. He asked me some questions and said that I should be taken to the ophthalmologic hospital in London for a check-up with specialists.

He called an ambulance which immediately took me, as I was, to the London Eye Hospital. When we arrived a group of doctors were waiting. They asked me questions and did a complete check-up. They asked questions about my life since my childhood. When they finished the check-up of my right eye, they asked me to come back to that hospital once a week because they wanted to study the case to come to a conclusion about what had happened to the optic nerve in the past in my right eye.

The ambulance took me back to St. Mary's Hospital in Paddington where I stayed a few more days. I went back to college and every week to the Eye Hospital. After three months the doctors came to their conclusion. "You had a rare infection in the optic nerve that causes blindness. One in a thousand is healed and you are one of them." And they continued, saying that the cause of the infection probably was a virus that was localized on the optic nerve since my childhood and manifested itself when I was a young man. It was all they could do for me and I did not have to come back again.

That day I came out of the hospital thanking God for what He does for those who trust in Him. (Psalm 37:5) "Commit your way to the LORD; trust in him, and he will act." I went back to college and continued studying. I knew I was guided by the Doctor of all doctors. It was He Who healed me. Praised be His blessed name! I was not walking alone, never alone.

In the second year of college it was compulsory for the students to visit churches and preach on Sundays, morning and evening. Every weekend I was scheduled by the college to preach in a church, most of the times outside London. This became a problem. I could not take Lucimar with me; we were not married! The church where I was going to preach prepared hospitality only for me, because at the college I was single. Because I had a scholarship, I had to be single to the end of my course. Lucimar also had been accepted at Abbey Christian School as single. We were in the situation that if we got married both of us would have to leave school, and we could not afford that.

The issue was that Lucimar could not travel with me on weekends, when I went to my preaching assignment at churches, some of them far from London; therefore, we could not see each other on weekends. We had no family in London; far from our home, it was a very unpleasant situation and we felt very sad since we couldn't see each other for a long time. I travelled alone and she stayed alone in London at the school.

We decided to get some advice from our friend Rev. Clifford Parsons, who spoke Portuguese and was pastor of Abbey Road Baptist Church, English teacher at the Abbey School and member of the board of the Baptist Missionary Society (BMS). I explained our situation and he understood it. He promised to discuss it with Dr. Murray, the principal of Spurgeon's College.

A few days later he came and told us what the principal had suggested: "João and Lucimar can get married, but João, in order not to lose his scholarship, will stay living at the college from Monday to Friday to continue his studies." And Pastor Clifford continued, saying, "Lucimar will move from the room at the school to the manse (with him and Lottie), working some hours every day in the house, and continue her studies at the school."

The manse, where the Parsons lived, was adjacent to the school. So, married, we could travel together to the weekend preaching. Unbelievable! But it happened!

We accepted the suggestion of Dr. Beasley-Murray and we chose a date for our wedding, which was April 3, 1971. We sent a message to our families in Brazil through a telephone call that took four days to complete. In those days, technology was not as advanced as today.

It was going to be just a very simple wedding, for we did not have the means for a celebration. We invited some Brazilian friends who lived in London, and we were very happy indeed when my class from college told us that they would prepare a reception for fifty people! They served tea, coffee and sandwiches. The School gave us a lovely wedding cake for the day and two to be sent to Brazil, to our families. Gerry Myhill, a friend from college, offered to take the photos. Rev. and Mrs. David Doonan offered me a beautiful English suit; Mrs. Lottie Parsons made Lucimar's bridal dress. The teachers from the schools decorated the church with beautiful flowers. Dr. Antonio Dutra, a pastor and psychoanalyst, a friend from Brazil, who was doing his PhD at London University, gave Lucimar away, representing her father, Victor Calvello. Sylvia Ventura, Lucimar's cousin, who was also studying at the School, was her bridesmaid. Rev. Clifford Parsons performed our wedding. While the Parsons were in Angola, Africa, as missionaries for twenty-five years, they had bought two cottages in Looe, Cornwall, England. They offered us two weeks in one of their cottages for our honeymoon.

The wedding ceremony was performed at Abbey Road Baptist Church. I rented a limousine to bring Lucimar, who was at the home of Peter and Joyce, our friends from the church.

After the ceremony, best wishes and pictures, we had a very nice reception at the school hall. My friends from college were superb to offer us this reception. Members of the church offered us some money for our train tickets that would take us to Looe, Cornwall. Jon Neal, a teacher at Abbey School and a good friend, taped the ceremony on a cassette tape. After the ceremony and reception Peter and Joyce took us to the Paddington Station to take the train to Looe, Cornwall, where we stayed for two weeks.

Looe is a small coastal fishing town in the southeast of Cornwall, thirty-two kilometres from Plymouth. Looe is divided into two small towns by the River Looe, East Looe and West Looe, connected by a bridge, with a population of five thousand.

Our special day, April 3, 1971

We stayed in the cottage "Amanha'. Clifford gave this name to the cottage because *amanha* in Portuguese means tomorrow, a very popular word in Angola, where people say, "Tomorrow we will work, not today; we leave everything for tomorrow; we don't work in a hurry."[41]

We visited Polperro, a large fishing harbour. It is a tourist town, located forty kilometres west of Looe. The streets are very narrow, built when there were no cars. In the past, Polperro was a centre of smuggling, products being brought from China. They were then sold to France and America. Back to Looe we went to an English pub called "The Jolly Sailor," where we drank a pint of Guinness.[42]

Next, we travelled by coach to Plymouth, where we visited the historic port from which the Pilgrim Fathers left for America on board the Mayflower in 1620. They were Puritan separatists from the Church of England who believed that a new start in the new world would be much better for them. They arrived in Cape Cod in December 1620. Because of their faith, they left their own land for another that they didn't know.

Our time in Looe, two beautiful weeks, had come to an end. On April 17, 1971, we took the train back to London. The train compartments had three seats on each side with the passengers facing each other. In front of us there was a very nice couple with whom we started a conversation, talking mainly about the weather, comparing it with the weather in Brazil, as we told them we were students from Brazil.

Finally, we arrived at Paddington Station, and back at Abbey School. The Parsons had prepared a very nice room in the manse, and there we started our married life. I could not stay living there because I had to go back to college, only coming back on Fridays. Every Friday I would go back to Abbey School, pass through Waterloo Station and buy Lucimar some beautiful tulips; Saturday afternoon we would travel together to the church where I was appointed to preach.

---

[41] See www.looe.org/.
[42] The founder of the Guinness brewery business, Arthur Guinness, was famous for his black bitter beer. He was also the Christian man who introduced Sunday School for children in Ireland.

14

&

ON THE BANKS OF THE LIS RIVER, LEIRIA, PORTUGAL

"A man without dreams is a man without life."
– Eça de Queirós

In May 1970, I received an invitation from a Baptist church, in Leiria, Portugal, to replace Pastor Antonio Martins, who was taking a leave of absence for four months. The pastor knew about me through Robélia, a Brazilian medical student who had been in London and knew the Leiria Baptist Church and its pastor. When she went back to Portugal, she mentioned my name to Pastor Antonio Martins, and he contacted me, inquiring about the possibility of my going to Leiria for four months. As I replied positively, the church sent me a letter of invitation and I travelled to Portugal at the beginning of June, when the college closed for holidays. It was an opportunity to help the church and the Portuguese Baptist Convention, to meet pastors and to travel in Portugal. I arranged with Pastor Martins for Lucimar to spend July with us in Leiria.

On my way to Portugal I spent two days in Madrid, Spain. There I stayed in a hotel very close to the famous Puerta del Sol (Sun

Gate). There came to my mind stories I had heard from my parents about people who left their country looking for better opportunities, especially in South America, because there was severe famine in the land.[43]

Following a travel guide I visited all the important tourist places, not forgetting the famous Museo del Prado, where famous paintings by El Greco, Goya, Raphael, Bosch and others were on display. I also walked around the Plaza Mayor, a major public space in the heart of Madrid.

I ended my visit to Madrid and left for Lisbon. I took the train, travelling all night and arriving early in the morning. I walked off the train, took my luggage, purchased a ticket to Leiria and waited until twelve noon, when the train left. In the history of Portugal, Leiria is a very important city. The area was dominated by the Moors until it was captured by Afonso Henriques, King of Portugal, in 1135. He built a castle to defend the area from Moorish invaders. Later King Don Dinis built his royal residence and settled in the town. He also ordered the plantation of the famous Pine Forest of Leiria close to the coast. The wood from this forest was later used to build the ships used by the Portuguese navigators.[44] I had the privilege of spending hours at the castle, reading and praying.

I arrived in the city in the afternoon, but no one was waiting for me. The problem was that the church was expecting me the next day. I had arrived earlier! I asked someone where the Baptist church was located, and I was informed that it was beside the firehall. So, I took my luggage and walked, asking here and there, where the firehall was. Finally, I arrived and there it was, the beautiful tall grey building of the Baptist Church in downtown Leiria. Of course, it was closed! It was Wednesday and I was informed that there would be a prayer meeting in the evening.

Then I asked a person who was passing by, "Do you know who the pastor of this church is?"

---

[43] Marília Klaumann Cánovas, *Hambre de Tierra: Imigrantes espanhois na cafeicultura paulista 1880 – 1930*, Lazuli, 2005.
This book (Land Hunger) describes very well the Spanish immigrants in the coffee plantation of São Paulo.
[44] *Wikipedia*, under the word "Leiria."

"Yes, it is Pastor Martins," he answered.
"Do you know him?"
"Yes, he is well known in town."
"Do you know where he lives?"
"He does not live in Leiria; he lives in São Pedro de Moel. It is a small village for tourists, on the coast," and he continued, "The church always meets on Wednesday; I am sure he will come for the prayer meeting."

I thanked him, and he left.

About eight o'clock Pastor Martins arrived. Some people were already inside the building, opened earlier by the caretaker. When Pastor Martins saw me, he came in my direction and I introduced myself, the student from Spurgeon's College. He was very surprised! He told me that he was expecting me for the next day. However, he was happy that I was there to start working with him at the church. He introduced me to the congregation, who were very happy that I had arrived. When the prayer meeting finished, we left by car to São Pedro de Moel, and arrived late in the evening.

My responsibilities at the church would be to lead the Bible study on Wednesdays, preach at Sunday morning and evening services and do visitation during the week as needed. I stayed at Pastor Martins' residence in São Pedro de Moel.

The history of the Leiria Baptist Church is quite interesting. A Portuguese couple, the Parreiras, who emigrated to Brazil, worked many years in Rio de Janeiro. There they went to a Baptist church and accepted Jesus as their Saviour and Lord. Their lives were transformed. Upon their retirement, they returned to Portugal to live in Leiria. As the city did not have a Baptist church, they started one and built, with their own money, the actual building that still remains to this day on Combatentes da Grande Guerra Street beside the firehall. They also invited a well-known Portuguese pastor who had just finished his studies at the Baptist Seminary in Rio de Janeiro, Pastor Antonio Maurício. Within a few years he worked as an evangelist and brought many people to Christ. The church grew and became large and influential in the city and in the Portuguese Baptist Convention.

When the Parreiras died childless, they left all their fortune, money and properties, that they had acquired while in Brazil to the Leiria Baptist Church with the condition that part of the money be used to build a home for elderly people. They also left instructions that some land on the coast close to São Pedro de Moel be donated to the Portuguese Baptist Convention to build a camp for young people's retreats. All this was done during Pastor Martins' ministry, and I had the privilege of visiting the home for the elderly and the camp.

Around Leiria there is a large pine forest known as the Pine Forest of Leiria or the King's Pine Forest. History says that it "was ordered to be planted by King D. Afonso III in the thirteenth century… between 1279 and 1325, increased substantially by King D. Dinis I… The pine forest of Leiria was very important in the Portuguese maritime discoveries because pine wood was used in the construction of vessels."[45] I walked, several times, along the trails of this pine forest observing the great height of each tree. I was amazed!

Almost every day I enjoyed taking a walk on the bank of the famous Lis River that runs across the city of Leiria dividing it in two, north and south. To rest my legs, I sat for a while close to the bridge. There is a museum that shows the history of Leiria and there are several restaurants. The Rio Lis is the charm of Leiria!

It was in Leiria, at the local library, that the Portuguese writer Eça de Queirós wrote his famous book *O Crime do Padre Amaro* (The Crime of Father Amaro), published in 1875. The novel is the story of a young priest, Father Amaro, who served in the Catholic Diocese of Leiria. Upon his arrival in Leiria he falls in love with the beautiful Amelia, the daughter of his landlady. Her fiancée, João Eduardo, exposes the local priest who was having sexual encounters with Amelia. His love affair with Amelia ends in tragedy when she becomes pregnant and is forced to seclude herself in the countryside and aborts the child. Amelia and the child both die. The church removes the priest to another parish and the crime is covered up.

In July, Lucimar came to visit me in Leiria. The day of her arrival, Daniel, Pastor Martins' son, took me to the airport in Lisbon. We went early so that we could visit Lisbon, getting to know the old city, built on the bank of the Tagus River. We visited the University of Lisbon, the Praça do Comércio, Rossio Square and other places.

---

[45] *Wikipedia,* under the words "Pinhal de Leiria."

We also went for lunch to a very nice restaurant, on the other side of the river. We ordered a seafood soup, codfish and a green wine.

Daniel left me at the airport and returned home to São Pedro de Moel. Lucimar was supposed to arrive about 6 p.m. from London. I sat on a bench to rest a little until the time came to welcome her, but the flight was delayed. So, I had to wait, but a few minutes later I began feeling sick, after a very rich meal. Lucimar had not come yet and I was informed that her flight would not come until midnight. I couldn't wait any longer. I took a taxi and asked the driver to take me to a hotel called Don João VI, in downtown Lisbon. Daniel had given me the address of this hotel, just in case.

As soon as I arrived at the hotel, I told the person at reception that I was not well; I might need a doctor, but, before calling a doctor, I asked whether he could bring me a strong cup of tea. I thought the lunch I had eaten was giving me indigestion. I took the cup of tea, went to bed, slept and woke up about five o'clock next morning. Then I remembered that Lucimar had arrived at midnight!

I paid the hotel bill, asked for a taxi, got into it and asked the driver to take me to the airport. I got there at 9 a.m., paid the taxi driver and ran in the direction of the airport lounge, where I saw Lucimar very worried, tired and not knowing what had happened to me. She had expected me to be there waiting for her. When she arrived and didn't see me, she looked everywhere in the airport, and, as she did not find me, she phoned Pastor Martins' house in São Pedro de Moel, "Pastor Martins, this is Lucimar speaking from the airport in Lisbon; I can't find João; do you know where he would be?"

Pastor Martins called his son to the phone.

"I left him at the airport, but if he is not there it is possible that he went to the hotel for which I gave him the address, just in case."

"Where is this hotel?"

"It is Don João VI; ask a taxi to take you there. It is possible that he may be sleeping."

It was past midnight! Lucimar went out of the airport, took a taxi and asked the taxi driver to take her to the hotel, in downtown Lisbon. There are many hotels downtown, but none with the name Don João VI. They went back to the airport and Lucimar waited there. She was very frightened thinking of what might have happened to me!

But I had not disappeared; I had almost died! Finally, we were together, we took a taxi and I told her all that had happened.

We arrived at the Lisbon train station and bought two tickets to Leiria, where Pastor Martins' daughter was waiting, and she took us to São Pedro de Moel. Everything was calm now; it was the beginning of a wonderful month.

Daniel, Pastor Martins' son, had recently come back from Portuguese Guinea, Africa, where he had served in the Portuguese Colonial War.[46] Daniel offered to take us on a trip to the North of Portugal. We visited Coimbra, with one of the oldest universities in Europe founded on the bank of the Mondego River in 1290. Coimbra has a well-known national forest called Choupal, not far from the city, where in the past the students from the university used to go for their musical leisure activities.

We walked among the Roman ruins of Conimbriga, the largest settlement in Portugal; we went through the Serra da Estrela (Star Mountain Range); we strolled in downtown Viseu, the city where the famous Renaissance painter Vasco Fernandes (known as The Great Vasco) was born, admiring this very important city, which probably is the birth place of the first king of Portugal, Afonso Henriques. We visited the Serra do Buçaco, where the Battle of Buçaco took place in which the French were defeated by the Anglo-Portuguese army, under Lord Wellington, on September 27, 1810. There is a historical monument at the site.

On our return we went through the city of Marinha Grande, an important Communist city, that fought against the dictatorship of António de Oliveira Salazar. I was in Portugal when he died July 27, 1970. It looked like a festival for many Portuguese people. I was seated on a bench in the main square of Leiria when a deacon from the church passed by and saw me.

He came close and asked, "Hi Pastor, have you heard that Salazar died this morning?"

"No," I answered.

"Yes, the dictator finally died, no more dictator."

"Oh, yes; is it good for Portugal?"

---

[46] *Wikipedia*, under the words Portuguese Colonial War, it "was fought between Portugal's military and the emerging nationalist movements in Portugal's African colonies between 1961 and 1974."

"Yes, yes, let's celebrate at the Tasca with a glass of good wine and have a conversation."

On the bank of the Lis River, Leiria, Portugal

As it was a Monday, my day off, I went with my friend to the Tasca. We spent some time there, happy that Portugal was starting anew quite peacefully. We left the Tasca, he went home and I walked back to the church apartment where I was staying at that time. A few days later I met the deacon at the church; he gave me a gift that I still have with me on the wall of my office. It is a beautiful painting with old English style words of Jesus saying to His disciples, "I am the way, the truth and the life" (John 14:6 GNT). This always reminds me of my time in Leiria, Portugal.

Lucimar and I spent a wonderful month together in Portugal. At the end of July, Lucimar travelled back to Abbey Christian School in London to continue her studies and work. I continued at the church in Leiria until September, preaching every Wednesday and Sunday in the morning and evening. During the week I visited families who belonged to the church. I also participated in several meetings of the Portuguese Baptist Convention.

Before I finished my time in Leiria, I wanted to visit the famous Shrine of Fátima, in the city of the same name. I went alone to see how the Roman Catholics worshiped the image there. I asked some people for information on how to get there. One of them told me that there was a bus that ran from a road north of Leiria. So, on a Monday morning I walked to that road and waited for the bus. I waited and waited, and, as it did not come, I started walking. Fátima is about twenty kilometres from Leiria. The bus never came! Then I noticed that Fátima was just in front of me, I had walked all the distance by myself.

It was a shock to see the amount of business just in front of the cathedral, the selling of small and big images of Our Lady of Fátima, candles and all kinds of paraphernalia as if they could heal everything on earth, when you kneel and worship in front of the image. The sadness is that it is done in the name of Christianity. They should read Exodus or Isaiah!

On that walk to Fátima I noticed that several farms were abandoned, and some houses closed. When I returned to the church in Leiria I enquired of some people why those places were abandoned. They answered that the owners had emigrated to Brazil, South Africa, Venezuela, the USA, France and Canada looking for a better life for their family.

A month before I left to go back to Spurgeon's College Pastor Martins called me into his office at São Pedro de Moel and revealed to me the main reason why the church had invited me to spend that summer in 1970 with them in Leiria. The church needed a full-time pastor. Pastor Martins couldn't be their pastor any longer, because he had other business in the tourism industry in São Pedro de Moel. So, he continued, "On behalf of the church I want to invite you to be our lead pastor."

I was greatly surprised at this invitation, because I was still studying at Spurgeon's College. I couldn't leave my studies in order to take a church in Portugal. So, after some time in prayer I answered the church that at that time I couldn't accept such a wonderful invitation. I could consider it when I finished my time at the college. I still had two more years of studying in my B.D. program.

September came and I went back to London. My time in Leiria, Portugal, was a very special and wonderful experience. I thanked God that he had given me that opportunity.

15

MEMORIES OF LONDON, ENGLAND

"The man who is tired of London is tired of life."
– Samuel Johnson

In college, life continued as normal, with a lot of essays to write, books to read and preaching on Sundays. I was taking the B.D. (Bachelor of Divinity) program of London University, which is equivalent to the M.Th. (Master of Theology) of the seminaries in the United States. Years later, when I came to London, Ontario, as a missionary of the World Mission Board of the Brazilian Baptist Convention, I submitted my certificates and diplomas from São Paulo Faculdade Teológica Batista and Spurgeon's College, London, England, plus the TOEFL[47] test of the English language from Western University, London, Ontario, to Eastern Baptist Theological Seminary, Louisville, Kentucky. The seminary granted me equivalence to their M.Th. program and was willing to accept me as

---

[47] Test of English as a Foreign Language

a student in their Doctor of Ministry program, but I had to live at the seminary for at least one year and then I could continue by correspondence (no Internet in those days!).

I declined because I could not leave the mission work and go with my family to a seminary. It was impossible! I thought I could do it by correspondence and travel to the seminary once in a while.

The years spent at Spurgeon's College were very difficult. Studying day and night for three years in a different culture and language and following lectures by English professors – these things were a great challenge. My studies were mainly in New Testament. I wrote several essays on the books of Oscar Cullmann[48], – *History of Salvation*, *Christ and Time* and *Parables of Jesus*. I also studied Dr. Beasley-Murray's book *Baptism in the New Testament*. This book became a classic on the subject of baptism. I learned to read in Greek Koine, the language of the New Testament.

Above all, the college emphasizes the preparation of each student for the pastoral ministry. It was a great privilege to be a student at such a prestigious school of theology as Spurgeon's College. My goal was to complete my studies, to go back to Brazil, to be a minister at a church and, if possible, to teach at a local seminary. In June 1972, in the tent erected in the courtyard of the college, I received my diploma. On that occasion, I was presented with several theological books, a special gift from the college. It was an immense satisfaction and joy. Lucimar was there with me and together we rejoiced.

Some days later, Dr. Beasley-Murray called me into his office. He encouraged me to continue studying the New Testament and informed me that the British Bible Society was offering me a Greek New Testament study book. The chairman called me to their headquarters at 146 Queen Victoria Street and offered me a copy of the New Testament in Greek Koine.

During my time at the college, I had several friends. Mike Elcome, the chair of our college class ("batch"), was a very good fellow. We still write to each other every Christmas. In 1982, when I

---

[48] Oscar Cullmann was born in Strasburg and studied philosophy and theology at the seminary there. He was a professor of New Testament studies at Basel Reformed Seminary and also at the Sorbonne in Paris.

was at Adelaide Street Baptist Church, London, Ontario, I suggested to the First Baptist Church, which was without a pastor and was looking for an interim, that they invite Mike to come for three months. He had taken a sabbatical leave and was interested in coming to Canada. The church invited him, and he and Caroline stayed with us, in our home, for three months. We had a wonderful time! John Wilthew, of Newcastle, was another wonderful friend, who always had time to listen to my stories about Brazil. He was a very good listener! Once, he invited me to travel with him to Newcastle for a weekend. It was then that we passed by the famous Newcastle football grounds, St. James' Park, and to this day I am a Newcastle United F.C. aficionado.

Another student, with whom I used to go for a walk after lunch, was John Dyer. We talked a lot about Brazil and the possibilities of ministry. When he finished college, he married Maria, and both presented themselves to the Baptist Missionary Society (BMS) for work in Brazil. They were accepted and worked there for many years until retirement. It was during his ministry there that he wrote his book *Finding God in Brazil*. We are still in touch, exchanging messages through the internet. Gerald and Joan Myhill were great friends and served as our wedding photographer! They, also, work in Brazil. Lucimar and I had the privilege of helping them to learn Portuguese.

June is the end of the academic year. College would re-start only in September. During the interval, I had to work to have some money to pay for our return tickets to Brazil. The first job was at the Inner London Education Authority. After that, I found a job at Peek Freans, a biscuit-making company. They were looking for someone who had come from a tropical country to take racks of biscuits to an oven heated to over 40°C or 104 °F. It was a temporary job, and I applied and was accepted. The biscuit-making company was founded by James Peek and George Freans in 1857 in Bermondsey, London, not too far from London Bridge.

As soon as Lucimar arrived in London, we went out a few times; I wanted to show her what I knew of London. London is wonderful! There are many things to see! Each stone has some history. Our first stop was Trafalgar Square. As soon as we arrived, pigeons from all directions came to meet us, looking for food. We visited the National Gallery, Westminster Cathedral, the Houses of

Parliament, Buckingham Palace, Tower Bridge, the Thames River and the London Embankment. Piccadilly Circus is the centre of London. I talked to some young people who were there, lying on the ground – hippies – smoking and playing guitar.

On one occasion when I went back to Piccadilly with a group of students from Abbey Christian School, one young lady with whom we had a conversation about the gospel wanted to go with us to the school. She went with us and the principal of the school accepted her and gave her a job. Barbara never returned to Piccadilly; she was converted, baptized and stayed in the school. It became her home in England.

Hippies at Piccadilly Circus

To live in London for four years was a gift from God. The English life, education and culture influenced the shape of my life.

We start our day with English breakfast; we learned to like rhubarb and enjoyed Yorkshire pudding and the delicious fish and chips which are more delicious when served in a cone made of the *Daily Mirror* newspaper! I learned to spend more time at the library, learned about cricket, and played at least once, and went with the students to a match at Lord's Cricket Ground near Abbey Road. I went several times, of course, to a football stadium to watch either Crystal Palace or Tottenham.

On our Sunday visits to churches, we felt at home worshiping God with our wonderful English friends. Even though it was a Baptist church there was a liturgy. The service, always starting with the reading of a Psalm, and the hymns accompanied by an organ touched my heart deeply. The preaching was always exegetical, which expresses much better the teaching of the text. Dr. Beasley-Murray always taught us that the best method of preaching is the exegetical and that we students should pay attention to the message that comes from using this method of exposition.

There are many churches in London. I visited the London Metropolitan Tabernacle, at Elephant and Castle, where Charles H. Spurgeon preached and was the pastor for thirty-eight years. During his ministry he organized many churches and founded the College and an orphanage. During World War II, the Tabernacle was bombed by the Nazis. A few years later it was rebuilt, and to this day it continues ministering the Word of God in London. I also visited, a few times, Westminster Chapel, where Dr. Lloyd-Jones, the great evangelical preacher, was the minister. The Assembly of the Baptist Union of Great Britain used to meet there. I visited Westminster Cathedral, at the centre of which is buried the great Scottish doctor, missionary and explorer David Livingston.[49]

During my time in college, two Baptist students from Russia were accepted to stay for three months. We had a wonderful fellowship and talked about the white Russians who immigrated to Brazil. They could not understand why I did not have to go every month to the Brazilian embassy to ask permission to continue studying in London! They had to go to the Russian embassy every month so that their passports could be stamped with permission to stay

---

[49] His heart is buried in Zambia Africa and his body in Westminster Cathedral.

one more month. Every month! With them I learned even more the value of living in a democratic society.

It was almost time to leave England and go back to Brazil to work somewhere where God would send us. Most certainly, there would be a place already prepared for us to serve in God's vineyard.

16

&

THE SS *PASTEUR*

"In my country there are palm trees,
Where the Sabiá sings fair;
And the birds, which here do warble,
Do not warble like those there."
– Canção do Exílio by Gonçalves Dias,[50]
translated by Frederick G. Williams

On June 16, 1972, we said goodbye to our friends from Spurgeon's College and Abbey Christian School. Rev Clifford and Lottie Parsons took us to Waterloo Station. Some other friends were already there waiting for us. The French liner company took our luggage from Dollis Hill and transported it to the port of Southampton.[51]

---

[50] Antônio Gonçalves Dias (born August 10, 1823, died November 3, 1864) was a Brazilian Romantic poet, playwright, lawyer and linguist. He wrote Canção do Exílio when he was studying at the University of Coimbra.

[51] We decided to go back by ship as the airfare was more expensive.

It was time to say goodbye to the friends who were at Waterloo Station. We embraced, cried and said *adiós* to all of them. We did not know when we would see them again. We boarded the train and waved to our friends; it didn't take too long until we were on our way back to Brazil. The train crossed a bridge on the Thames River, from which we could see the great city of London, and shortly we were travelling through small towns built along the railroad in the direction of the port of Southampton.

Time had gone quickly; four years had passed since we arrived in London. Now, we were going back. I was wondering all the time where God would send us to start our ministry. At the same time, I knew that God was in control and He had a place for us somewhere in Brazil. He always has the best for those who trust in Him. As a "big bee," diligence was part of my life; that was why I had come to this point. I was always determined and diligent and put all my effort into the realization of my studies. God always helped me and Lucimar to reach that which we had worked hard to accomplish. And from that moment on it would be the same, as there is no success without those qualities. The bees are example for us to imitate. They are symbols of hard work. We were ready to work with diligence in the position where God would put us.

From a distance we saw Southampton. It is an important and well-known city in England. The *Titanic* left from here for New York. Its builders, Harland and Wolff of Belfast, Ireland, thought that, because it was a big and strong ship, nobody could destroy it, not even God. However, on its first trip it struck an iceberg off the coast of Newfoundland on April 15, 1912. An estimated 1,500 people died.

We left the train and we were already at the port. To our surprise Rev. Michael and Gill Wotton were there waiting for us. They lived in Bournemouth, where he was the local Baptist pastor. They came to be with us in the moments before the ship left. The *Pasteur* was waiting to board the passengers who were going to Argentina and Brazil. Meanwhile, we had a wonderful time of fellowship with the Wottons. We had spent a wonderful weekend with then earlier in the year when I had the privilege of preaching at his church. They also were planning to go to Brazil as BMS missionaries[52].

We didn't wait too long. We had to say goodbye to our friends. We boarded the ship, and were taken to our cabins; we entered, put our hand baggage on the bed and found beside it a vase with one dozen beautiful red roses. There was a card wishing us a good trip and the blessings of God upon us. It had been sent by Abbey Road Baptist Church and Abbey Christian School. We were so happy!

The *Pasteur* was a luxurious ship with forty-one years of history, built for the French shipping company Compagnie de Navigation Sud-Atlantique. It travelled from Europe to Rio de Janeiro, Santos and Buenos Aires. During the Second World War, when France was occupied by the Nazis, the ship was taken over by Great Britain and it carried thousands of troops between Canada, South Africa, Australia and South America. It was in this ship that we went back to Brazil with stops in Le Havre (France), Vigo (Spain), Lisbon (Portugal), Rio de Janeiro and Santos (Brazil). We learned at that time that it was the last trip to South America.

It was a wonderful trip. Going back to Brazil in a ship was not

---

[52] They went to Brazil and had a great ministry in the city of Curitiba, where Lucimar and I met and helped them with the Portuguese language.

in our plans. However, by air it was much more expensive. Pastor Clifford Parsons suggested it to us as he had gone by ship to Africa many times.

We went for our first dinner and took a table where we could watch the ship sailing on the Atlantic Ocean. The food was delicious! After dinner we walked on the promenade around the pool, and later we sat in the ship lounge where we could see the great ocean and the dolphins swimming, accompanying the ship.

Later we moved to a table in the bar, joining a gentleman whom we had met before. He was from England, but was at that time living in Cordoba, Argentina. It is a big city 700 kilometres northeast of Buenos Aires. He and his wife were returning from holidays in England. They had a ranch in that region. He had already drunk more than sufficient. While we were there, he never stopped drinking. He talked a lot and shared about his life in Cordoba. He liked Argentina, but also missed England. It is quite interesting that, when a person leaves his own country to live in another, he loses his identity. He loves the country he lives in, but never forgets the motherland. And all the time he keeps on saying that next year he will go back for good, but for fifty years he keeps on saying it again and again. Globalization can't explain this! We live in a globalized world, but no one can explain that feeling which is inside the hearts of the emigrants. My friend was drinking more and more and became emotional about missing his motherland.

Time was passing and it was dark. We said goodbye and left for our room. I spent quite a long time thinking about so many emigrants who leave their country to have a better life in another country, thinking that they are going to a promised land of milk and honey, and suddenly discover that there is no milk or honey, but only hard work and not enough money. The ship started rocking. We were crossing the Bay of Biscay, in the direction of Le Havre, France. The ship rocked all night, although we slept a little bit. Next morning during and after breakfast we heard several stories from people who reported that they were afraid and thought we wouldn't make it. The sea continued to be rough with great waves rolling up and down and the ship still tossing somewhat.

Le Havre is a city located in the Normandy region of northwest France, at the mouth of the Seine River. It is a very important port. A man from San Francisco, who was travelling the world and with whom I became acquainted on the ship, came with us to visit the city. Downtown Le Havre was totally destroyed during World War II, but it was reconstructed by the famous French architect Auguste Perret[53]. We walked all day until late in the afternoon, at which time we went back to the ship. In the evening the *Pasteur* left Le Have for Vigo in Spain.

Two days later we arrived in Vigo, Spain. I was very happy to visit Spain once again as I had visited Madrid on my trip to Portugal. Vigo is a city in the Galicia region, a very important port in Europe and a very old well-kept city. Lucimar and I walked all day in Vigo. I was trying to buy gifts for my mother and father, who were born in Spain. When you don't have very much money it becomes very difficult! Finally! I found a sombrero for my father and a *leque* (fan) for my mother. They were souvenirs from Spain.

The next day we left for Lisbon, Portugal. It didn't take too long to arrive in Lisbon. The ship docked at the Praça do Comércio (Commerce Square) a symbol of the great Portuguese ships that travelled all over the world discovering new lands. We went out to visit the city, the Belém Tower and the Cathedral and we also went for a coffee at the famous Café a Brasileira (Brazilian Coffee House), a traditional coffee house in Lisbon at the Largo do Chiado. It was founded in 1905 and became a famous place for several Portuguese writers such as Fernando Pessoa (1888-1935), to whom a statue was erected in front of the Café.

After two days in Lisbon we left for Rio de Janeiro. It was a long journey of eight days on the sea. We usually enjoyed sitting after coffee at the bow of the ship watching the sea and the dolphins and reading. I took several books but didn't read very much. Next day as we looked far into the distance, we saw land and we were told that it was the Azores.

I talked to a few people who were going to Buenos Aires. One of them told me that he was a farmer in Argentina. He told stories of his life when he arrived for the first time in that country and how

---

[53] Auguste Perret (born February 12, 1874, died February 25, 1954) was a pioneer in the architectural use of reinforced concrete. He designed a group of buildings in the centre of the port of Le Havre.

difficult it was to start a new life in a foreign country. One day he asked me whether I liked soccer (football in England).

"Yes," I answered.

He, then, started telling me about the soccer teams in Argentina. Many clubs were founded by English immigrants – Racing Club, River Plate, Boca Juniors, Newell's Old Boys and others.

Every night there was dancing in the bar. We didn't participate except the night when the ship was going to cross the imaginary line that marks the equator and divides the northern and southern hemispheres. That night we received a certificate for crossing the equator.

One day we were informed that we were travelling in Brazilian water. In the distance we could see the Fernando de Noronha archipelago. It is a protected national marine park and ecological sanctuary, with undeveloped beaches and good for scuba diving and snorkeling. At dawn the following day we arrived at the Baía da Guanabara (Guanabara Bay). From afar we saw the beautiful Rio de Janeiro, Sugar Loaf Mountain, Corcovado Mountain (with the Christ the Redeemer statue) and the beautiful beaches of Rio. What a fantastic view at the dawning of a new day! That morning will stay in our memories as the most beautiful picture we had ever seen.

The *Pasteur* arrived in Rio. We all went out for a short visit to Rio de Janeiro. I called our friend Pastor José Reis Pereira, the editor of *O Jornal Batista* (the Brazilian Baptist newspaper). He then asked us to go to his office, which we did. There he took a picture of us to print in the paper and invited us to go for lunch at his house. That day we ate delicious Brazilian food, with Brazilian dessert, dried fruits and guava with fresh cheese. We talked about our stay in England and our future in Brazil. I told them that I had an invitation to teach at the Faculdade Teológica Batista in São Paulo.

After lunch he took us for a tour of Rio, and then we went back to the *Pasteur*, where we waited until it departed for the last part of our trip, the port of Santos. We arrived in Santos, the same port where my grandparents had arrived years earlier, on the *Espagne*.

Early in the morning of June 30, 1972, the *Pasteur* was navigating the waters of Santos. We were anxious to see our family, who were waiting for us at the port. Soon we were embracing each one of them, who also were anxious to receive us after four years away in England.

We had a wonderful reception at the home of my sister Carmen and brother-in-law Euclides. We stayed at my mother's house for a while until we decided where to go to start our ministry. I went for a meeting with the director of the seminary in São Paulo from which I had an invitation to teach New Testament. Pastor Werner Kaschell offered me fourteen hours of teaching, but that was not enough to live in a big city like São Paulo. Besides, I had been influenced by the English culture and I looked more English than Brazilian. When I met my friends who were already ordained ministers, they would comment about my looks! So Lucimar and I prayed about this – whether it was the will of God and whether God was showing us another place to go. It was at this time that I received another invitation from the Baptist Theological Seminary in Curitiba, where several English missionaries were working. We didn't know any people in Curitiba, except Rev. David Doonan, the same missionary who had introduced me to Spurgeon's College. The seminary offered me part-time teaching but also accommodation. We felt that it was a good place to start our ministry in Brazil.

MINISTRY

17

THE LAND OF THE ARAUCARIA TREES

"Do not be wise in your own eyes;
*fear the L*ORD*, and turn away from evil."*
– Proverbs 3:7

Upon our return to Brazil, we started a new life in Curitiba,[54] in the State of Paraná, in August 1972. Pastor David Doonan was the interim director of the Baptist Theological Seminary in Curitiba. He gave me support as I was beginning as a teacher in the seminary and also awaiting a call from a church in Curitiba. I taught in the morning and evening. The seminary prepared students for the pastoral ministry. At the end of four years of studies they received a Bachelor of Theology (B.Th) diploma.

---

[54] Curitiba is the largest and capital city of the State of Paraná, in the south of Brazil, with a population of 1.7 million inhabitants. It is surrounded by many araucaria trees, a variety of evergreen native to South America.

First Baptist Church was waiting for a new minister who was coming at the end of year, Pastor Marcílio Gomes Teixeira. The deacons approached me asking whether I could preach at Sunday morning services. I accepted the invitation and for about three months I preached in that church. I enjoyed very much that time at First Baptist Church as I was just arriving back from England and needed some time of adaptation until I had my own church. The church then asked for my ordination. The Association of Curitiba Baptist Churches gathered together with several pastors and, on October 9, 1972, I was ordained. The preacher for that occasion was Rev. Tony Bourne, a BMS missionary in Brazil, who was one of my friends.

I continued preaching on Sunday mornings for a while and teaching New Testament at the seminary, waiting for an invitation from a church in Curitiba. There were several churches that were looking for a pastor.

Lucimar and I wanted to live in Curitiba, at that time a colonial, calm place, starting to grow and becoming an industrial city. It was then that we helped two BMS missionary couples to learn Portuguese – Gerry and Joan Myhill and Keith and Barbara Hodges. Keith and Barbara didn't stay too long in Brazil as they moved to Portugal with the same mission. Gerry and Joan worked for many years in Nova Londrina, a town in the State of Paraná, until their retirement.

Lucimar wanted to continue studying; so, she took a course in methodology to teach English as a second language. She taught private lessons at home.

There was an American Consulate in Curitiba. One day an American missionary, Rev. Bill Damon, who also was a teacher in the seminary, came to me enquiring whether Lucimar would be interested in working at the consulate. He said that the American consul was going to call her, and he did. Lucimar went for an interview and was hired for the position of assistant to the consul, as she spoke excellent English and Portuguese.

A few days later the consul was looking for a translator for an American executive who was coming to help a company, called Prosdócimo, that was doing research to start a chain of supermarkets in Curitiba. I was invited and accepted to work only afternoons for three months. I worked with Mr. Moler, visiting every supermarket and looking for land where a new store could be opened.

When I finished my time with the consulate, Mr. Moler suggested to the owner, Dr. Jaime Prosdócimo, that he hire me to be a full-time employee. My answer was very clear and firm: "It was an excellent experience to work for you, but God called me to be a pastor, and for this reason I can't accept such a superb invitation."

Two years later the consulate in Curitiba was closed, and then Lucimar was invited to move to Brasilia to work at the American Embassy. They offered her a great salary and an apartment for us[55]. However, Lucimar did not accept the invitation because I was called to be a pastor and she would continue beside her husband.

One morning Rev. David Doonan came to see me and let me know that the Prado Baptist Church was looking for a pastor and was going to give me an invitation. The church asked me to preach for a call. I preached at Sunday morning and evening services. It didn't take too long for an invitation to arrive in my office at the seminary. Lucimar and I prayed and felt that I should accept the invitation to be their pastor. I was inducted into Prado Baptist Church, 599 Comendador Roseira Street, on November 11, 1972. The church could not pay me very much; so, it was agreed that I would continue teaching at the seminary.

To my surprise, as soon as I started the ministry at Prado, I noticed that the church was divided into three groups. One group left the church for unknown reasons, others didn't want to have a lead pastor any longer and others were supporting the new pastor. I prayed and started a visitation to every member family of the church. First, I wanted to visit those who had left to invite them to come back. One of the leaders was a military man. On a cold, dark winter night, a deacon and myself went to visit him and his wife. We were received very well by his wife. She made tea for us and we waited for a long time until he came to the sitting room. Apparently, he didn't want to see us!

When he came, he was very surprised that I was there with the deacon, exactly the one with whom he had had some problems in

---

[55] Not many people wanted to move to Brasilia as it was very difficult to live there.

church meetings. And then I told him and his wife, "We are here tonight because we believe that God brought us to your home."

"Yes, but," our brother answered, "I am not in the church any longer, I am not going to that church anymore."

"Your help in the development of the church is very important," I said. And then I reminded him that he was a great leader and had helped the church so much for so many years. The congregation admired him very much and liked his teaching in the Sunday school.

Prado Baptist Church young people's retreat

When I finished my talk, I asked him whether he would like to say something else or ask a question. He said that he would think and pray and wouldn't say anything that night. I knelt and prayed for that brother, his family and the church. We left that house giving thanks to God that He always works for good to those who trust in Him. That brother and his family were among the first to arrive for the following Sunday morning service. He never left the church again.

It was at this time that I discovered that the church had a big problem to be solved. They had bought a parsonage (manse) for the previous pastor in a very good subdivision of Curitiba. Those days the bank didn't give mortgages to churches. So, the pastor, with the permission of the church, bought it in his name, but the church was paying for it. The mortgage was for thirty years. When the pastor left, the church continued paying monthly, but the house continued being under his name. It was a very unpleasant situation that had to be solved. To resolve it the church had to pay the entire principal in order to transfer the documents into the name of Prado Baptist Church. It was too much money for the church to pay. They did not have the money.

Every Sunday we heard people complaining about it. "The financing costs are too much."

"We will never be able to pay for the house."

"We will lose the property."

"It is impossible."

It was a material thing that was affecting the spiritual life of the church. We prayed for wisdom to face the problem. We read in Ecclesiastes 10:10b that "wisdom helps one to succeed." It was exactly what we needed at that time. Wisdom was what all of us wanted to have. Every family in the church was asking what to do and how we would raise money to pay the bank. We continued praying for God to give us ideas and wisdom to solve the problem.

One morning in my office at the church, as I was praying about the situation God gave me a solution. In my vision I saw the church people working together, doing their best in order to raise money to pay the mortgage that was bringing so much worry to all of us. On Sunday morning I preached on Numbers 13:1-16. After walking forty years in the hot desert the Israelites arrived very close to the promised land. Moses, then, chose twelve men to spy out the land and bring a report. They spent forty days spying out the land, went to Hebron and to the fertile Wadi Eshcol where they cut down a branch with a single cluster of grapes, and carried it on a pole between two of them.

When they returned two reports were presented to Moses – one positive and one negative. The negative was that "… the people who live in the land are strong, and the towns are fortified and very large; and besides, we saw the descendants of Anak there. The Amalekites live in the land of the Negeb; the Hittites, the Jebusites, and the Amorites live in the hill country; and the Canaanites live by the sea, and along the Jordan" (Numbers 13:28-29). But Caleb had a different view, a positive view. "Let us go up at once and occupy it, for we are well able to overcome it… If the LORD is pleased with us, he will bring us into this land and give it to us, a land that flows with milk and honey" (Numbers 13:30b and 14:8). Victory depended on the relationship that they had with the Lord, their God.

That morning I suggested to the church that each one of us make a special effort to raise money to pay our mortgage completely and that this depended on our relationship with God through Jesus Christ our Saviour. We had to walk by faith like Joshua and Caleb. Victory would be achieved, the problem solved, and the church would continue doing its most important task, which was to preach the gospel and to be the presence of God in the midst of the community.

I also presented to them a plan that God had put in my heart. To raise money in a poor community is not easy. The people of Prado Baptist Church were very simple working people, but they were ready to do their part, to make their contribution.

First, we would take an offering among the members.

Second, we would challenge the Paraná Baptist Convention to loan us half of the mortgage.

Third, we would do a walkathon. We would ask our relatives and friends to support each person who walked. Seventy-five people volunteered to walk twenty-five kilometres. It was a big challenge, but with God many things are possible. We raised more than enough and paid the mortgage, and the house was transferred into the name of Prado Baptist Church. It was a wonderful victory and we celebrated it with gratitude to God for what He had done for us. From that moment on, the church started growing and the ministry continued in that area of Curitiba.[56]

It was in Curitiba that our first son, Victor, was born on my thirty-second birthday.

---

[56] The money the church borrowed from the Convention was paid in full in one year.

18

PRINCESS OF THE FIELDS

*"For who is God except the L*ORD*?*
And who is a rock besides our God?"
– Psalm 18:31

In September 1975 I accepted an invitation from Frist Baptist Church in the city of Ponta Grossa, in the State of Paraná, a region known as the Princesa dos Campos (Princess of the Fields). It is the third largest city in the state, at a road junction between the State of Paraná and the State of São Paulo, a busy and prosperous city. It has a university, an industrial park and a military base, that of the 13th Armored Infantry Battalion.

We moved into the manse, and I was inducted as senior minister of the Ponta Grossa First Baptist Church on September 25, 1975. Representatives of the Baptist Convention, the city and the ministerial association were present to welcome us.

Ponta Grossa First Baptist Church is one of the oldest Baptist churches in the State of Paraná. It was founded on December 3, 1923. I had a very busy ministry at this church as it had 650 members with seven small congregations. Four of them outside and three inside the city. It was the responsibility of the pastor to visit them and make sure that the leadership was doing its ministry. I preached or taught five times on Sundays – two services, teaching new converts, a radio program and young people's evening meetings. The church was well known and respected in the city

Together with the deacons we organized a program of visitation in the city. We made sure that every family who had left the church was visited and invited to come back to the flock. I organized thirteen cell groups with six teachers trained by the pastor to give lessons every week in homes. We also started a Winter Institute every July, with hundreds of local young people participating. We organized a youth choir and an orchestra as I discovered several people in the church who could play instruments. A member of the church, an immigrant from Russia, used to be a conductor in his own country and I challenged him to organize the orchestra. He was very happy, and it was a great blessing. Once a month there was an orchestral Sunday evening service. As a result of all these programs, I was privileged to baptize one hundred eighty people.

First Baptist Church, Ponta Grossa, Paraná, Brazil

Ponta Grossa is a city with a great spiritism influence[57], which is very well spread all over Brazil. The local Spirit Care House used

---

[57] Spiritism (also called Kardecism) is a spiritualistic philosophy and religious movement started in the 19th century by the French educator Allan Kardec.

to invite me to bring a message to their annual meetings. They always wanted me to talk about love. Several of their members were professors at the local university.

The general of the 13th Armored Infantry Battalion was a Christian. He always invited me to be present at all their military ceremonies, representing the Ponta Grossa ministerial association, of which at that time I was the chairman. Sometimes he even asked me to pray. I could not refuse for in those days we were living under a military junta government!

Our second son, Daniel, was born in Ponta Grossa in 1976.

In 1977 I was chosen by the Brazilian Baptist Convention, which was meeting in Curitiba, to be a member of the Junta de Missões Mundiais (World Mission Board). So, beyond my activities in the church and in the Paraná Baptist Convention I also had to travel to Rio de Janeiro every three months for meetings of the World Mission Board. It was in one of these meetings that I heard a report given by Rev. Fanini about the need for missionaries in Canada. He spoke for a while in our meeting in Rio about how many immigrants from Portugal and other countries had made the city of Toronto their new home. Baptist churches in Ontario were receiving people in their services who could not speak English and they wanted to do an outreach in the communities. They needed pastors with a background in the Portuguese culture who could communicate with these new immigrants.

As I spoke Portuguese, Spanish and English and had some experience with Portuguese culture and as I had worked in Leiria, Portugal, Lucimar and I started praying about this challenge. After a while we felt that we could help in the mission work in Canada. It was a joint project with the Department of Canadian Mission (DCM) of the Baptist Convention of Ontario and Quebec (BCOQ). We felt that God had a plan for us for the next few years in Ontario, Canada. We wrote to the JMM (World Mission Board) in December of 1978 expressing our call and desire to work in the project of the DCM and JMM in Ontario, Canada.

19

&

ON THE BANKS OF THE OTHER THAMES RIVER

"Go from your country and your kindred and your father's house to the land that I will show you."
– Genesis 12:1b

After several interviews in the office of the World Mission Board of the Brazilian Baptist Convention in Rio de Janeiro, we were accepted in March 1979 to work in London, Ontario, Canada. I informed the First Baptist Church of Ponta Grossa that we had been accepted for the mission work in Canada. Of course, they were somewhat surprised, but understood that we had to follow what God was saying to us at that moment.

Immediately I went to the Canadian Consulate in Rio to apply for an immigration visa, which would be the proper way to work in Canada without any problem. I was informed that the Immigration Department at that time was in Buenos Aires. We had to wait for an officer who would come to Rio in August to interview the candidates for immigration to Canada. I was informed by the secretary of the Canadian Consulate that we could go to Buenos Aires, Argentina, and apply from there, thus speeding up the process. The second option was better for us because we had to arrive in Canada no later than September.

With the permission of the World Mission Board I immediately set up an appointment with the immigration officer at the Consulate in Buenos Aires, Argentina.

When I arrived at the consulate I was interviewed promptly. I had taken all the documents from the Baptist Convention of Ontario and Quebec, the documents from the Brazilian World Mission Board and my own. After examining all of them the officer said that he had to interview Lucimar as well; she was not with me. So, I went back to Ponta Grossa and returned with Lucimar the following Monday. She was interviewed, and the officer told us to wait for our visas in Rio[58]. They would be sent to the World Mission Board address.

As we were in Buenos Aires, we had the opportunity to visit some important places like Florida Street, the governmental palace Casa Rosada (Pink House), Praça de Mayo and other areas in downtown Buenos Aires.

The next day we flew back to Ponta Grossa, via Curitiba. I informed the church that we would leave for Rio at the end of June. The church prepared a farewell service for the last Sunday of June, in which Pastor Boyd Williams, a BMS missionary, preached. After the service coffee and cakes were served while we said goodbye to all who came that night. It was a very emotional time and also a time of gratitude to God and to all the people of the First Baptist Church for four excellent years of ministry in that city.

A few days later we started sending our books to London, Ontario. At the end of June, we travelled to Rio, to the offices of the World Mission Board. While in Rio we stayed at the Colégio Batista (Baptist School) until our documents from the Canadian Consulate arrived from Buenos Aires. While we waited, we took the opportunity to visit Rio with the family. We went to the beach several times, to the Christ the Redeemer statue (Corcovado Mountain) and Sugar Loaf Mountain and I also preached at several churches.

---

[58] Joe Clark, the Conservative Party leader, had just been elected the Prime Minister of Canada. His picture was already posted in the Consulate in Buenos Aires.

We received our immigration documents and travelled to Toronto on September 16, 1979, in a Boeing 707, with a stop at John F. Kennedy Airport, New York. Before our departure in Rio we went to the airport chapel to pray together with Rev. Waldemiro Tymchak, Executive Secretary of the WMB, Rev. José Reis Pereira, Chairman of the WMB, and a friend of Rev. João Keidann and his family, who were already in Toronto at Olivet Baptist Church as missionaries of the WMB in partnership with DCM.

We were on our way to London, Ontario, to be Associate Pastor at Adelaide Street Baptist Church, which was surrounded by a large Portuguese community, mainly people from the Azores. Our mission in Canada would start there.

The flight was wonderful, but we were tired. The children, Victor and Daniel, were quite happy. When we arrived in New York, in the morning of September 17th, the USA immigration did not let us into the country. Our flight to Toronto was from LaGuardia and we had to enter the USA and transfer to that airport, but we were not allowed to do so. However, the USA officers were very polite and took us to a room where we stayed for a while, until they arranged transportation for us with a USA officer, who drove us to LaGuardia Airport. I had never thought that we needed visas to go through the USA in order to change airports!

Waiting for us at Toronto Pearson International Airport were Rev. João and Glaucia Keidann of Olivet Baptist Church; Roy and Mae Taylor, Chairman of the Deacon's Board of Adelaide Street Baptist Church, London, Ontario; Rev. Horace Estabrooks of Olivet Baptist Church, Toronto, Ontario; and Lembit and Asta Willik, friends we knew back in Brazil and now residents of Toronto. We stayed at the Keidanns' residence; they were very kind to host us for a week.

On our first Sunday in Canada we were introduced in the morning service at Olivet Baptist Church. I had an opportunity to say a word explaining about our coming to Canada and the mission that we had in front of us, to which God had called us at Adelaide Street Baptist Church, London, Ontario, a century-old church in downtown London which at that time had about eighteen thousand Portuguese people. The church wanted to do an outreach mission in that community.

Sunday afternoon a caravan from Olivet Baptist Church took us to Adelaide Street Baptist Church, London, Ontario, which was waiting for us. We were introduced to the church in a special afternoon service. It was very meaningful to us. We felt the support of all the English and Portuguese speaking people who came to welcome us. We felt the presence of God and His direction for our lives. We were never alone. He was guiding us, and we were obedient, walking in the same direction He had shown us. It was a wonderful service and reception, the beginning of a great missionary journey in Canada.

Roy and Mae Taylor took us to their home, where we were received as family. They hosted us until we found a house to rent. They treated us very well and received our children as if they were their grandchildren. Victor, Daniel and Marcos used to call them Grandma and Grandpa; in fact, they were the only grandparents they knew. Those days at their home were a time of learning about life in Canada. The children were anxious to see snow and were always asking when it would come. It took a long time, but finally one morning when we woke up it was all white outside. A beautiful picture! We went out, all of us, to experience touching the snow with our own hands; it was soft, like cotton, but cold. We went quickly back inside as we learned that you don't stay out too long when snow has fallen, and the temperature is in the minus Celsius part of the thermometer. After a few months we really started to learn about the winter in Canada – grey, cold, very cold, with a lot of snow and freezing rain, very long and requiring care when you walk outside. Our first winter in Canada looked like it would never come to an end.

London is a city located the southwest part of the Province of Ontario, about two hundred kilometres from Toronto. In 1793 the land was chosen by Lieutenant-Governor John Graves Simcoe for the capital of Upper Canada. This idea didn't work out, but the district of London was founded and populated by Europeans between 1801 and 1804 and London became a district town in 1826.

I wrote an article for our Brazilian Baptist newspaper *O Jornal Batista* in which I mention my first impressions of London, Ontario: "Because it is a city with just over a hundred thousand inhabitants it does not look like the millennial London, England. London, Ontario, is new, modern and different. However, as we get familiarized with it, we notice that there are some similarities. The river crossing the city from east to west has the same name, Thames River. Some places are called Hyde Park, Piccadilly or Waterloo. There are several parks and the flowers are delicately taken care of, as in London, England. In the fall the colours are unequaled in every part of the city, making the Londoners happy and preparing their spirits for the long, cold, grey winter that is coming."

Like London, here too there was a church on every corner. There were seven Baptist Convention of Ontario and Quebec (BCOQ) churches. The Adelaide Street Baptist Church, one of the oldest churches in the city, at one hundred and three years old, on the corner of Adelaide and York Streets, was well known by the Londoners. It was a church that was in decline, but was hopeful that a Portuguese ministry would revive the ministry in downtown London. The church, through the Department of Canadian Mission, invited us to come start the Portuguese ministry of which the main emphasis would be outreach in the Portuguese community that surrounded the church. I was provided with a small office. It was in that office that I wrote my first prayer letter to the Baptist churches in Brazil.

Our first Christmas in London, we organized a small program at the church on December 23, 1979. Lucimar prepared some children for a small presentation called "The Message of the Angels and the History of Christmas." The children were wonderful!

In the beginning it was very difficult; only a very small group of Portuguese people were coming to the English services, and most of them did not speak English. Even though we had spent four years in England and spoke English, still we had to go through some adaptation to the Canadian and Azorean culture. We didn't have too much knowledge of the Azorean people, especially of when and why they came to Canada. I had to do some research about them and learned that most of them immigrated to Canada in the fifties and seventies.

My induction into the Portuguese ministry of Adelaide Street Baptist Church was on February 3, 1980. The chairman of the Middlesex-Lambton Association, Rev. David Ogilvie, performed the induction and Rev. Ron Harmer presided at the service.

I started the ministry organizing an intense visitation to the Portuguese homes in the vicinity of the church. The Portuguese people follow a very traditional Roman Catholic religion taught to them by the Church. Most of them go to Mass just on special occasions like infant baptism, Easter, the procession of saints and Christmas. They know the traditions of the Church, but not much about Jesus. The emphasis in our ministry was to teach those who welcomed us who Jesus is and why He came into this world, through Bible studies. I also got involved in the multicultural centre's orientation of the Portuguese immigrants who arrived in London, wrote to the local Portuguese newspaper and the immigration department of Canada, did translation in hospitals and did visitation in the business area.

Portuguese ministry orchestra and congregation, London, 1984

Even though it is not easy to talk about the gospel with Portuguese Catholics – and I learned how difficult it is – we were blessed with many accepting us into their homes and listening to our explanation of the gospel, using their own Catholic Bible. They preferred to call me a "Baptist priest" and not "Pastor." There were always those who wanted to hear more about God and Jesus. A girl said to Lucimar, "I hope to go to church every Sunday."

As soon as I started the ministry in London, Ontario, I learned four biblical principles that helped me to walk in the direction that

Jesus guides – love, patience, persistence and prayer. Without the application of these principles in our lives it is impossible to do ministry. They are fundamental in missionary work. I had to practise them in my own life. I learned them from Jesus Himself, Who came into the world to show love toward us. He was compassionate. In His ministry He practised patience and He was persistent, even with His disciples. He also prayed and taught us to pray. Luke recorded Jesus praying seven times in his gospel. So, in the ministry, we are called to imitate Jesus; He left an example for us (1 Peter 2:21), because He was the One who called us to this ministry.

I had the privilege of helping to start other Portuguese ministries. I was invited to go to Montreal to help Madison Baptist Church and to encourage them towards a Portuguese ministry. Montreal at that time had an estimated sixty thousand immigrants from Portugal. I also helped the Spanish congregation in Montreal to purchase another building, with finances from the BCOQ.

On June 22, 1980, the Portuguese ministry at the First Baptist Church of Strathroy, Ontario, started. At least one-third of the population of Strathroy came from the Azores. For about five years I walked alone through the streets of that city praying that God would open a door through which I could enter to explain the gospel. God heard my prayers and not just one door was opened but a few doors. I then started a Bible study in those homes. Soon we had a congregation, and, with the support of the church, the DCM and the World Mission Board, a missionary couple, Rev. Jackson and Noemi Rondini, and their three children, came to work in Strathroy.

In July 1980, from the 8th to the 12th, the Congress of the Baptist World Alliance met in Toronto, at the Maple Leaf Gardens. Many Brazilian pastors and lay people participated in it. Lucimar and I went to some of the meetings. Our church, Adelaide Street Baptist Church, supported one pastor from Brazil, paying his expenses to come to the Congress. Pastor Altair Prevedelo and his wife came and stayed in our home. He was the executive secretary of the Paraná State Baptist Convention.

During the Congress we had a special meeting of pastors:
Rev. José Reis Pereira, editor of *O Jornal Batista*;
Rev. Waldemiro Tymchak, executive director of the World Mission Board;

Rev. Archie Goldie, executive secretary of the Department of Canadian Mission;

Rev. Horace Estabrooks, pastor of Olivet Baptist Church, Toronto;

Rev. João Keidann, pastor of the Portuguese ministry, Olivet Baptist Church;

Rev. João Garcia, pastor of the Portuguese ministry, Adelaide Street Baptist Church, London.

The issue that brought us together was to discuss and establish a method of doing Portuguese ministry in the Baptist churches of Ontario. It was clear that the missionaries did not come to Canada to start Portuguese-speaking churches. They came to help the established English churches to do outreach in the communities and to integrate mainly the children and young people into the English congregation and at the same time to have a Portuguese service, for those who spoke only Portuguese.

On July 13, 1980, the last day of the Congress, a caravan of 150 Brazilians travelled to London, Ontario, where we had a wonderful celebration at Adelaide Street Baptist Church. It was a bilingual service, the symphonic choir of the Baptist Seminary in Recife, Brazil, sang and the preacher was Rev. Valdívio Coelho from the First Baptist Church in Salvador, Bahia, Brazil. After the service the church offered a delicious dinner for four hundred people at the country club, whose owner was David Melo, a member of the Portuguese ministry. Several people from the community and Western University were present at our celebration.

Our third son, our Canadian son, Marcos, was born in late 1980 in London, Ontario.

In the second year of our missionary work in London, we planned to organize a Portuguese choir. We were a small group who liked to sing. So, we got together to plan a cantata for the Christmas service. Some young Portuguese people didn't speak Portuguese very well, but were willing to help. I challenged a lady from the English ministry, who played the piano very well, to help us with our small choir. Mrs. Bev Barret accepted our invitation, even though she didn't speak a word of Portuguese. From September on, every Friday night the choir got together for rehearsal. In the beginning everything went well. Everyone was faithful, on time, learning the words in Portuguese and learning the music.

Ministry

My job was to promote, in the Portuguese community, the cantata and the program that we would have at Christmas-time at Adelaide Street Baptist Church. I went out many times inviting people, talking about our choir in the business area, in the streets, in houses door to door. People were very excited to know about our choir and we were expecting many to come for the service at Christmas. However, close to the event Mrs. Bev Barret felt tired and discouraged and she resigned. She didn't come any longer for rehearsal. We felt very sorry for her, but we had a problem. We were in the situation that we could not cancel the service or dismiss the choir. We had to continue and pray that God would perform a miracle and send someone who could speak Portuguese, knew music, could conduct a choir and was willing to help us. Only God could do this in such a short time!

I called on the church to pray. Only God could save the Christmas celebration with the Portuguese choir. It would be a big disappointment for the missionary work in London to cancel the program, as the whole Portuguese community was excited to come to listen to a Portuguese choir. All of us were praying that God would send us a new director for the choir, and soon.

One Sunday morning, just after starting the service, I saw from the pulpit a young man entering the sanctuary and sitting in the last pew. I had never seen him before. I didn't know who he was. I finished the service and walked to the door to greet the people as they left the church. That young man was the first that I greeted as he was seated in the last pew. I thanked him for being present at the service and then asked him whether he lived in London. He answered that he was a student at Western University and spoke Portuguese. Then I invited him to come for lunch in our home. He accepted and after I had greeted everyone we went home; I was not even thinking about the choir and our great challenge. Lucimar and I were very surprised and happy that a young man at the university spoke Portuguese.

On our way home he made an observation about my driving. "Pastor, you drive like a Brazilian; go fast and stop suddenly!"

"Yes," I said, "I live in Canada, but I haven't forgotten the Brazilian way of driving."

And then he said, "My parents were missionaries in Recife, Pernambuco, Brazil."

"Well," I said, "that is great; how long were they there?" I asked.

"I am not sure how long, but a few years with the South American Mission," and he continued, saying that he lived with them before coming to Canada to study.

We arrived home. We came in and, as he sat in the living room, he saw that we had a piano. He stood up went to the piano and started playing it beautifully. Lucimar and I were amazed at his ability to play, how he moved his fingers on the keys.

"Who plays?" he asked.

"Lucimar," I answered.

Then he told us why he was now living in London. "I am studying music at Western University. I am specializing in choir music. I am in my last year of the Bachelor of Music."

I stood up, as I was sitting on the sofa, and came close to the piano, where he was plying. Immediately I thought that God was answering our prayers.

Lucimar called us for lunch. We sat at the kitchen table and prayed and I continued talking to our guest friend. I told him about the situation with our choir at the church. I asked him whether he could help us, directing our choir, to prepare for a Christmas cantata.

"Yes," he answered, "I would be very happy to do that," and then he told us why he was at the church that morning. "I woke up this morning with a deep desire to go to a church service. I had breakfast and left, driving my car without knowing where to go to worship God. When I passed in front of Adelaide Street Baptist Church, the white church, I noticed on the sign that there was a Portuguese service at that time. Immediately I felt that it was there that I should go. I drove into the parking lot, parked my car, got out and went into the church and straight into the service. I sat down and paid close attention to the pastor, who was praying, asking God to help with the choir's situation. At that moment I understood why I woke up that morning with a deep desire to go to church."

I introduced that young man to the choir the following Friday. They were very happy, delighted and relieved at the solution that God had given to us for the choir. After some rehearsal we could notice how much better the choir was singing. Christmas day came and we had approximately 250 people from the Portuguese community in our celebration. It was a beautiful service, where the gospel was preached, reminding the people why Jesus came into the world. The choir sang beautifully, and the young man directed it with mastery. Praise the Lord, a real miracle!

After the service we had a time of fellowship, coffee, tea and cakes. The church offered the young man a gift of money. I was busy talking to people. When I wanted to say thanks to that young man, I looked for him everywhere, but never found him. He disappeared with the same mystery as he had arrived. For me there was no doubt that God had sent us an angel to help us in the circumstances that we were going through. Praise God that He answers our prayers. We are never alone; He leads us. Jeremiah said to the people of Israel that when they look for God he will be found: "When you search for me, you will find me; if you seek me with all your heart, I will let you find me, says the LORD" (Jeremiah 29:13-14a).

For almost eight years the missionary ministry to which we were called was done in London, Ontario. Lucimar and I worked intensely to organize, to grow and to integrate the Portuguese people into the established Canadian Adelaide Street Baptist Church. In June 1981 I wrote a prayer letter to the World Mission Board and the Baptist churches in Brazil in which I said:

"In the midst of many difficult situations, with love, patience, persistence and prayer, God gave us the great victory of seeing the English congregation recognize that the Portuguese young people and children are new Canadians and they don't speak Portuguese. Therefore, they needed to be integrated into the English congregation. We were very happy that more than fifty young people and children have been accepted into the English congregation."

We had as organist in the Portuguese ministry a wonderful Canadian lady, a member of the English congregation. She moved with about thirty other families to a new congregation that was starting on Wonderland Road, Westview Baptist Church.

We no longer had an organist. It was then that Lucimar decided to learn to play the piano better in order to be the Portuguese ministry pianist. She studied a few hours every day with the help of a teacher. Soon she was playing and she helped us in London and also in Oakville, where she played for twenty-one years. We praise God that Lucimar was willing to diligently sacrifice herself and learn to play the piano.

A few times we organized the Portuguese Easter Conference in London. We always had a wonderful meeting with lots of people. This conference was started in 1978 with Rev. Dionísio Pape in his church, King Street Baptist Church, Cambridge, Ontario. At Easter 1979 Rev. Dr. João Keidann, a Brazilian Baptist missionary at Olivet Baptist Church in Toronto, was the invited preacher. In 1980 the invited preacher was Rev. João Garcia, who had arrived at Adelaide Street Baptist Church in London in September 1979. The Easter Conference continues to be a great blessing to the Portuguese people. They faithfully come every year to the Easter Conference wherever it is being celebrated.

During my time in London I was involved in the Middlesex-Lambton Association of Baptist Churches. In 1987, when in Oakville, I was invited to help the Department of Canadian Mission and to visit multicultural churches. I had the privilege of travelling anywhere from Montreal to Windsor visiting churches and their pastors.

During the school break in March of 1981 our family went to Louisville, Kentucky, to visit the Southern Baptist Theological Seminary. Dr. Lewis Drummond had been my professor at Spurgeon's College and he had invited us to go for a visit. He was a professor of evangelism. He also wrote an extensive biography of Charles Haddon Spurgeon.

Marcos, our youngest son, was four months old. Before we travelled to Louisville, a sister from the Portuguese ministry insisted to Lucimar that she would take care of Marcos during our time away. We both agreed and left him with this wonderful couple.[59] On Saturday they went to McDonald's for lunch. On the way they had an accident. A fast truck on the wrong side of the country road caused his car to go out of control and crash. Marcos was safe, protected by the car seat. People who saw the accident thought that he was dead, but he was alive and well, praise the Lord! The car was totally destroyed. The truck continued its trip as though nothing had happened. Josué came out of the car asking for Marcos. When he heard that he was well, he knelt on the road and gave thanks to God that He had saved them all.

---

[59] Brother Josué and Inês da Silva, who lived in Paris, Ontario

In the summer of 1981, we started a mission project in Lincoln Park, Detroit. A Brazilian couple, who knew about our mission, travelled to London to meet me and asked whether I could go to Lincoln Park at least once a month. The Portuguese congregation of London, Ontario, plus the choir, travelled to Lincoln Park Baptist Church for the inauguration service. It was a missionary trip, the beginning of a new mission work. We did that ministry for more than a year. Lucimar and the children came with me the last Sunday of every month. However, we felt that was not our priority, and started looking for another pastor who spoke Portuguese and English and who could continue that mission.

Then the English congregation of Lincoln Park called the Southern Baptist Home Mission Board, who decided to take over that project. The Detroit area director of the Home Mission and I travelled together to Louisville, to visit the Baptist seminary and interview a Brazilian pastor studying there, to determine whether he could be invited to take over the mission at Lincoln Park. We met Pastor Walter Santos and presented the challenge to him. He had to travel from Louisville to Detroit every weekend. He accepted the invitation and I had the privilege of inducting him into that ministry.

We continued our mission work in London, Ontario. Several families were added to the church and soon we had a wonderful group of Portuguese people worshiping God at Adelaide Street Baptist Church, the white church on Adelaide Street as it was called by the Portuguese community.

It was a very difficult time when the English ministry decided that they couldn't continue supporting our ministry any longer, and decided to cease to be, sell the building and scatter to other churches in London. The reason was that the church was not growing and they could not pay the bills; besides, thirty families had left to start Westview Baptist Church. That happened in the summer of 1983, when I had to travel to Brazil on furlough.

A pastor who worked for the Department of Canadian Mission (DCM), Rev. Dan Dryer, was invited to come to visit the church and give some advice on the matter as we, the Portuguese congregation, were trying to help the church not to close; we were surprised at his advice; he said that the church should be happy to close because it had given birth to two other congregations, Westview and the Portuguese church. And he continued, saying that the Portuguese congregation should look for another place to continue its ministry. At the final meeting the Portuguese congregation abstained from voting. The church was sold to an Independent Baptist ministry that had been in London for a while.

We were all very sad, and I travelled to Brazil with this in my mind, praying and asking God for direction. When we returned, I got a copy of the *London Free Press* from Monday, June 27, 1983, with the article "After 106 Years of Worship, the Final Blessing." The journalist said that "the death of Adelaide also marks a new beginning for Westview," but did not mention the Portuguese ministry, which probably was not important. I had no idea what he meant by "blessing." For us it was a time of mourning and nothing to do with blessing.

The Portuguese ministry had to face reality and decide whether we were to continue or whether I would return to Brazil. After some meetings and long discussions, every member was willing to continue the mission in the Portuguese community of London and area. All we had to do was to find a new place for the ministry. We tried several other churches, but no one was willing to take what was for them a large group of Portuguese people, especially because we had too many children and they had insufficient teachers. One church said that they did not have enough parking space, and another gave us a list of fifty things we couldn't do in their church building.

It was based upon those negative reactions from sister churches that we decided to buy our own building. We searched in the Portuguese area and we found a ceramic factory for sale, which could be renovated for church purposes. At the same time an effort was made to prepare the people to see their responsibility in contributing to this project. At one memorable Sunday service, every family brought a special offering envelope. That morning, we raised almost thirty thousand dollars in cash, plus a cheque for two thousand. It was very clear that God was giving us that building. We bought it for $105,000 and started the process at city hall for changing the city by-laws. The area was designated for business purposes, and we had to ask for a modification to use the building for church purposes. It took longer than we thought, but finally after two long meetings the city decided in our favour.

The renovations would cost us more than we anticipated. We needed al least another $100,000 to do all that the city required from us, to renovate for religious services. We did not pay for the people who were willing to do the work. At that time of year – winter – Portuguese people do not work and thirty-two men, including people from the Catholic community, helped us do all kinds of work. That was a great blessing from God!

We had to raise more money as the congregation did not have any in the bank. So, with the permission of the Middlesex-Lambton Association, I wrote a letter to every church and the Department of Canadian Mission explaining our situation. We raised close to the one hundred thousand dollars needed to do the renovations. The project was started in January 1984 and by April everything was done. We celebrated, dedicating the church building to God on May 20, 1984. At the special service we had representatives from the Olivet Portuguese ministry, Rev. Bira da Silva; from the Department of Canadian Mission, Rev. Albert Coe; from the World Mission Board of the Brazilian Baptist Convention, Rev. Waldemiro Tymchak; from several Baptist churches of the Association; and from the real estate company that sold us the building, Mr. Euclides Cavaco. We offered a trophy to each person who had worked on the renovation and a plaque was put on the social hall of the building.

It was a great service of thanksgiving and rejoicing for all that God had done for us. The preacher invited to bring the message for the occasion was Rev. Waldemiro Tymchak, who spoke about the importance of preaching the gospel everywhere in the world, not forgetting the multicultural mission. After the service a delicious meal was served to all present.

The ministry continued, now in the new building. Lucimar became the new pianist for the services. We organized an instrumental band with six people, four playing saxophone, one flute and one guitar. It is interesting that three of them were Catholics! They played in our service and then they played for the Mass in the Portuguese Catholic church. The church continued to grow, and we had a wonderful group of children and young people. The Sunday school had at that time 65 children and young people enrolled.

We came to a point where we needed a youth pastor as we had a special ministry to the Portuguese young people. We met every Wednesday for Bible study and prayer. These young people thought they should have a youth minister for their meeting and start an English ministry with the Portuguese church. A proposal was presented to the church and after days of discussion it was decided to ask for support from the Department of Canadian Mission and the Association. Both approved our project and were willing to help. It was now for the church to vote and help financially. This was done in a meeting called for this purpose. There were more than seventy members present. A long discussion took place; some were in favour and others against. Then the vote was called, and the result was amazing; a very telling number of votes were against it. A few votes more were in favour of the youth ministry. I thought that with this result it would be very difficult to work with a congregation having two views on such a very important issue, the youth ministry.

In a meeting of the leaders in October 1986 I felt that the Portuguese people preferred to have a ministry only in their own language. I suggested to them that they invite a minister who would do the ministry only in Portuguese. Then immediately after the meeting I went home and together with Lucimar, and in prayer in the presence of our God, I wrote a letter resigning from the pastorate of the Portuguese Baptist Church in London, Ontario.

The letter was read in the morning church service, Sunday, November 9, 1986. I informed the World Mission Board of the Brazilian Baptist Convention that I was resigning from the ministry of the London Baptist church. The Mission Board acknowledged my resignation and through its secretary, Rev. Waldemiro Tymchak, suggested that we should go to teach at the Madrid Bible School. I thought that was an excellent idea. We continued praying and I did research about the Baptist convention of Spain and their Bible school, and I was thinking of travelling to Madrid to visit the school. However, I received a letter from the World Mission Board explaining that the leadership in Spain wanted me to go first to plant a church in a given city in Spain, and then after three years I could go to teach at the Bible school.

Lucimar and I prayed about this suggestion and decided that the best thing at that moment was to go back to Brazil, to work with the Mission Board, visiting churches and talking about the mission in Canada, and then to decide whether we would come back or stay in Brazil.

20

&

FROM SADNESS TO JOY
(From Baca to Beracah)

*"Happy are those whose strength is in you,
in whose heart are the highways to Zion.
As they go through the valley of Baca
they make it a place of springs;
the early rain also covers it with pools."
– Psalm 84:5-6*

The Hebrew word *Baca* is a derivation of the verb to weep, to cry, to shed tears. The pilgrims, who came from every direction, on the way to Jerusalem for the religious festivals passed through this valley of Baca. It was well known as a dry valley. So, when they arrived at this place and did not find water, they cried and poured out their tears; they cried with sadness. At the same time, going to Jerusalem, they transformed it into a place of joy and hope because they knew that they would be very happy celebrating the festival in the presence of Jehovah at the temple. A valley that, even though it was dry and sad, was transformed into a valley of joy and hope.

The Hebrew word *Beracah* means blessings. The feeling of sadness as they did not find water was transformed into a valley of blessings because they were headed in the direction of Jerusalem. They were very happy because they were the people of God. Joy took the place of sadness. This speeded up their journey in the direction of Zion, where, finally, they would worship the truly real God Jehovah. "They go from strength to strength; the God of gods will be seen in Zion" (Psalm 84:7).

The psalmist, many times, showed this change in feelings that happens only to those whose eyes are fixed on God.

In 2 Chronicles 20 we read the impressive account of the great blessing King Jehoshaphat received from God, in the battle against three kings who came together to fight against Israel. Jehoshaphat became very worried and depressed thinking that there was no way out of that situation. It was his "valley of Baca," valley of tears, through which he had to pass, like the pilgrims to Jerusalem. At this precise moment in his life, he had to look to God, Who can transform any desperate situation, that apparently has no solution, into a hopeful and happy situation.

After victory against his enemies, following the instructions of Jehovah, the Lord God, Jehoshaphat and his people met at the Valley of Beracah, the valley of blessings, to celebrate the wonderful victory. God had transformed his valley of Baca into a valley of Beracah.

As missionaries of the World Mission Board and the Department of Canadian Mission of the Canadian Baptists of Ontario and Quebec, Lucimar and I went through a situation with the Portuguese ministry in Adelaide Street Baptist Church, London, Ontario, similar to the pilgrims who were on the way to Jerusalem. We also had to look to God and trust in Him Who can transform the impossible into possibility and, therefore, sadness into joy. We are not always prepared for these situations; therefore, in the midst of our fear we look to God, Who always answers our prayers, teaches and guides us, and we follow Him, which results in blessings to us, individually and as a community. We are never alone; He is present and encourages us when we walk through the valley of Baca and changes the situation to a valley of Beracah. The valley of sadness and tears is transformed into a valley of joy and hope.

It is difficult to understand how a church comes to this point of selling its building and ceasing to be! I tried to get at the logic of what had happened. All explanations that were given to me did not answer my question of why the church had to close its doors. At that moment all I saw was that the Christian people who worshiped God in that building lost their missionary vision towards the community where it was located.

This was our valley of Baca and we had to go through it, a dried valley, of tears and sadness. So suddenly the Adelaide Street Baptist Church, that had existed for more than a hundred years, one of the oldest churches in the city, where we had our Portuguese ministry, decided to accept an offer to purchase the building and ceased to be. In the month of June 1983, the church ceased to be, closed its doors and finished all activities and the ministry in London, Ontario, was *finito* (done).

Lucimar and I looked to God, and the Portuguese congregation did the same. We were on the street and needed some direction. What were we to do? God always gives us wisdom when we look to Him. He always answers our prayers. The Portuguese ministry at the Adelaide Street Baptist Church had grown from just a few people, who came to the English services, to become a majority on the membership roll. We could, with our membership, influence the decision and stop the sale, but after several meetings of the Portuguese congregation it was decided that the best way was to abstain from voting and leave the issue with the English congregation. After all they were long-time members of the church.

The reasons that led the church to take such a decision were written in a letter that the English congregation sent to the World Mission Board of the Brazilian Baptist Convention. First, the church was composed mostly of retired members, and, therefore, aged people who were no longer prepared to do the ministry of evangelism. Second, the church had organized another church on the west side of London with a group of about fifty people who had left Adelaide. Third, the church was starting to have financial problems.

The Portuguese congregation knew that the ministry should be done in the middle of the community. Then we began looking for another church that could take our congregation. With the advice of the Department of Canadian Mission, we approached several Baptist

Convention churches, but it was quite difficult for them to take us for the following reasons:

> One said, "You have many children and we don't have enough teachers."
>
> Another said, "We don't have enough parking."
>
> Another gave us a list of fifty things we could not use in the building; and
>
> One just said, "We are not interested."

So, we had to make a decision whether to continue with the Portuguese ministry or to go back to Brazil. I called a meeting and explained to the Portuguese members that if we stayed and continued with the ministry we had to organize the church as a Portuguese Baptist church, to buy a building, to become a member of the Middlesex-Lambton Association of Baptist Churches, to write a constitution and to register with the Government of Canada for tax exemption purposes.

After long discussion and prayer, the decision was that the missionary family should stay and organize the church. They also promised to contribute financially toward buying a building in the Portuguese community's area of London. They were happy that, from then on, they would make their own decisions as an autonomous church. At the same meeting the first leaders were chosen. They also took the bold decision of choosing three delegates who, with the pastor, would look for a church or a building to buy to serve as the Portuguese Baptist Church in London. As we could not stay where we were this was the proper way to go, in faith, united and ready to help. In that meeting, we all made a promise that every Portuguese family belonging to the church would contribute financially to this purpose. So, I informed the Department of Canadian Mission of the Baptist Convention of Ontario and Quebec and the World Mission Board of the Brazilian Baptist Convention about what was happening and both boards approved and were praying for us.

It was determined that in two weeks from that meeting we would collect a special offering in the morning service. One week before, envelopes were distributed among all members of the congregation. I spent a great amount of time in prayer looking to God for wisdom and direction. My verses from Scripture were Psalm 25:4-5, "Make me to know your ways, O LORD; teach me your paths. Lead me in your truth, and teach me, for you are the God of my salvation; for you I wait all day long."

It was a beautiful day that Sunday morning. We went to the service with great anticipation, thinking of what God had spoken to the Portuguese people. The offering was taken at the end of the service. Three leaders were chosen to take the envelopes from all of the families and count what they had offered to God. With one exception all brought cash, offerings to help to buy a building for the Portuguese ministry. At that memorable Sunday morning service, the people gave twenty-nine thousand four hundred dollars plus a cheque for two thousand dollars. It was a miraculous proof of faith. All members were saying, "Let us continue with this blessed ministry." It was the will of God that we continue forward; He would always be with us. It was a story to be told to our grandchildren!

After walking for a while in the community with a real estate person we found a place. It was a ceramic factory, recently built, in the centre of the Portuguese community, at 501 Nelson Street. The owner told us that she could not continue to work making ceramics. She had to retire! She told us that another church had tried to buy the property, but didn't because the city had too many requirements in order to change the area bylaws. However, we thought that God was giving that building to us and we had to do all we could to have the bylaws changed. If the church members would vote to buy that property it would be the Portuguese Baptist Church of London, Ontario.

I called a meeting for Wednesday after our prayer meeting. We had an extraordinary meeting and the vote to buy the ceramic building was taken. All were in favour! Thanks be to God; we were very excited. The price was one hundred and five thousand dollars, which was paid with the offering given by the members of the church plus a loan from the bank. God had transformed our sadness – valley of Baca – into happiness – valley of Beracah. Like the people of Israel who still had to travel to arrive in Jerusalem, we too had to walk until the building could be renovated to be used for church purposes.

As soon as we closed the deal, we went to the city hall, with our lawyer, requesting a change to the bylaws in that area, which was designated for business purposes. We wanted the designation to be changed to allow religious purposes. It took two meetings for the city council to vote in favour of the change. On January 16, 1984, they voted unanimously to change the bylaws and allow the Portuguese Baptist Church to be established in the area. We felt the presence of God in that decision and we praised Him for leading us in the process. We were never alone.

The following Sunday we celebrated with a service of gratitude in which Psalm 84:5-6 was read by all the congregation:

"Happy are those whose strength is in you,
in whose heart are the highways to Zion.
As they go through the valley of Baca
they make it a place of springs;
the early rain also covers it with pools."

We also read Psalm 89:5:

"Let the heavens praise your wonders, O LORD,
your faithfulness in the assembly of the holy ones."

We then started the renovations. The city asked us to follow every requirement of the provincial construction codes. We had to spend more money than we had budgeted, but we had promises from churches of the Middlesex-Lambton Association that they would help us financially during the renovations. We praise God that every church sent their contribution and we had enough to finish the renovations, which were done by thirty-two volunteers, and some wonderful faithful women prepared delicious food for all of us. The Department of Canadian Mission also contributed with a very good cheque, sent when we most needed it.

After all renovations were done, the church building of the Portuguese Baptist Church in London, Ontario, was dedicated to God. The Portuguese newspaper of Cambridge, Ontario, *The Lusitano*, published on its front page an article about the inauguration of the Portuguese Baptist Church in London, Ontario, written by Rev. Dionísio Pape, pastor of the Preston Baptist Church in Cambridge. He wrote as follows:

"On Sunday May 20, 1984, there was a religious celebration in London, when the Portuguese Baptist Church was dedicated to the service of God. The church building is located in the centre of the city, at 501 Nelson Street, in the Portuguese community. Before the service started, the beautiful church building was already full, and many people were in the rooms adjacent to the sanctuary, as it was a great number of people who came to the inauguration service. The dynamic pastor of the church, Rev. João Garcia, started the service reading the

Holy Scriptures and praying. Several visitors were introduced, among them Rev. Waldemiro Tymchak, who is the executive director of the World Mission Board of the Brazilian Baptist Convention. Also present was Rev. Ubirajara da Silva, the new pastor of Olivet Baptist Church in Toronto. Several Canadian pastors spoke for the occasion, congratulating the new church. The young pastor Isaque Amorim represented the Cambridge Portuguese Baptist Church. Rev. Alberto Coe, the executive secretary of the Department of Canadian Mission, of the Baptist Convention of Ontario and Quebec, preached the inaugural sermon, interpreted into Portuguese by Rev. João Garcia. After the service a delicious lunch was served by the women's society of the church."

21

ON THE SHORE OF LAKE ONTARIO

"The secret of those who triumph is to start all over again."
– Author unknown

Before we travelled to Brazil in December 1986 I was invited by the deacons of Central Baptist Church and Rev. Jack Anderson to go to a meeting at Central Baptist Church in Oakville, Ontario. Lucimar and I came from London without knowing too much about the town or the church. We arrived early so we had the opportunity to visit Oakville. Then we found out that it was the richest town, based on income per capita, in Canada. We parked our car on the shore of Lake Ontario, downtown. We prayed about our future asking God what He had for us in the near future. We still had not accepted the invitation of Central Baptist to come to start a Portuguese ministry.

The objective of the church was to start such a ministry as it was surrounded by a large Portuguese community. I was informed that Portuguese was the second language most spoken in Oakville. Many families lived not too far from Central Baptist. It was a great opportunity to start a Portuguese ministry. The deacons and a very good number of members were ready to approve such a ministry. The Department of Canadian Mission and the World Mission Board were behind it and would provide financial support and Rev. João Garcia was the pastor to be invited to come to Central Baptist Church and start this ministry.

In that meeting I explained to the church that, if invited, I would use the same model as that used in Olivet Baptist Church, Toronto, and Adelaide Street Baptist Church, London. I informed the deacons that the World Mission Board did not send missionaries to Canada to start ethnic churches, but to help the established Canadian churches to reach out into the Portuguese community with the gospel. They came with knowledge of the culture, costumes and Portuguese language, to go out and be the presence of Christ in their midst. The Portuguese people came to this country as immigrants and made Canada their promised land, even though some of them always thought of going back to the Azores.

The best method of doing such mission was to work together with the already established Canadian church. The missionaries were to be associate pastors to the senior pastor of the church. It would be a ministry and not a new church. The new converts and those who would come from other Portuguese-speaking churches should be accepted as members of Central Baptist. It would be, therefore, only one membership, with two services (one in English and one in Portuguese), one Sunday school in English and only one youth group in English. The offering taken in the Portuguese ministry would be put together with the offering of the English congregation, and the church would have only one budget. In this budget would be included a new item, Portuguese Ministry. An annual amount would be approved for expenses of the new ministry. The Department of Canadian Mission, the World Mission Board and Central Baptist Church would support the invited missionary family. This method was approved by all present at the deacons meeting in December of 1986.

On December 13, 1986, we went back to Brazil, where we stayed for five months working with the World Mission Board, which rented an apartment for us in Campinas, São Paulo. Our task was to visit Baptist churches in the State of São Paulo informing them about the mission in Canada and the work of the World Mission Board. As we visited churches, one of them, a large church in the city of

Araçatuba, First Baptist Church, approached me with the intention of inviting me for the senior pastor position. Araçatuba is a very big and rich city in the northeast area of the State of São Paulo. The church has a great ministry with a great potential of expanding. Lucimar and I prayed about it and had a meeting with our boys to check their thoughts. When we told them that we had such an invitation they all started crying that they wanted to go back to Canada. "We wanted to go to Canada; we don't want to stay in Brazil."

Nevertheless, they had a wonderful time in Campinas. We lived in an apartment building where there were several Brazilian children; our boys made friends with them and, instead of playing soccer as is the custom in Brazil, they soon were teaching them to play hockey, the favourite sport in Canada. They used brooms as hockey sticks!

One day as I was walking in downtown Campinas thinking and praying about staying in Brazil or returning to Canada, I entered into a Catholic book shop and, by chance, I saw a bookmark on which was written a phrase that caught my attention and helped me decide to accept the invitation of Central Baptist Church to start a Portuguese ministry. The phrase was, "The secret of those who triumph is to start all over again."

Those five months in Campinas were excellent for our children. They enjoyed that time very much, had fun, met their granddad, grandmother, cousins, aunties and uncles, but we had to go back to Canada! I accepted the invitation of Central Baptist Church. Lucimar and I were very clear about what God wanted for us in the next few years. He was giving us a great and difficult challenge, to start a new Portuguese ministry now at Central Baptist Church, Oakville, Ontario. A new city, church and community and new relationships. We never walk alone; God was with us all the way.

The Portuguese ministry at Central Baptist started on Sunday, May 1, 1987. We were introduced at the morning service by Rev. Jack Anderson. My official induction took place Sunday, June 21, 1987, at three o'clock in the afternoon. The leader of the service was the chairman of the Toronto Baptist Association, Rev. Gordon Walker; the preacher was Rev. Robert Wilkens, the executive secretary of the Department of Canadian Mission; the title of his sermon was "Committed to Mission"; Rev. Jack Anderson introduced the Garcia family, Rev. João Garcia, his wife Lucimar Garcia, and the children

Victor, Daniel and Marcos; Rev. John Keidann, senior pastor of Kipling Avenue Baptist Church, Toronto, inducted the new pastor; Rev. Flávio dos Santos, senior pastor of King Street Baptist Church, Hamilton, delivered the induction prayer.

A difficult task was in front of us, but we knew that our lives were in His hands and, therefore, we were not alone. I wrote a letter to the World Mission Board, which was sent to the Brazilian Baptist churches, saying, "We are resting in the Lord because 'we abide in the shadow of the Almighty'. (Psalm 91:1b) We came back to Canada to a city called Oakville, located in the greater Toronto area, on the shore of Lake Ontario. We will extend our ministry into Brampton and Mississauga, two other cities close to Oakville, where more than four thousand Portuguese people live."

In May 1987 the Portuguese ministry started with only the missionary family. I really did not know where the Portuguese people lived. So, I searched in the telephone book – Portuguese and English. I wanted to know where they lived in Oakville. It didn't take too long to have a list of one thousand five hundred addresses. We assigned them to the right side and left side of each street in Oakville. All the addresses were recorded in an address book that I left in the office. The secretary of the church also put all the addresses into the computer in Portuguese files. So, when I drove on one given street, I knew in which house a Portuguese family lived. That way we could send invitations for special meetings at the church. I also wrote a bulletin, *Boas Novas*, that was distributed to every house three times a year, at Christmas, Easter and the church anniversary. Our goal was to be a presence of the gospel in the community and let them know that we wanted to show the love of Jesus, serving as much as we could. Soon I was being called to take people to hospital and doctors and translating for the Halton Multicultural Council, schools, the Ontario provincial social assistance ministry and the Halton Police probation officer. Central Baptist Church was fulfilling the teaching of Jesus, recorded in Matthew 25:40, "Truly I tell you, just as you did it to one of the least of these who are members of my family, you did it to me."

As our ministry was at the beginning and would take some time to develop, the Department of Canadian Mission invited me to help at their office in the area of multicultural ministries. So, for two years I went to the Baptist Church House offices, at 217 St. George

Street, Toronto, every Wednesday, and also travelled when necessary anywhere from Montreal to Windsor visiting multicultural churches and their pastors. I was assisting Rev. Bob Wilkens and Rev. Keith Cooney, the area minister for Montreal. I was a translator, in the Portuguese and Spanish languages, and counselor for those pastors who were coming to Canada to work with the Baptist Convention of Ontario and Quebec. At that time many people were coming from Nicaragua, El Salvador, Guatemala and Cuba asking for political asylum, and I was able to help on behalf of the Baptist Convention through the Department of Canadian Mission. Many had to leave their countries in a hurry and come to an unknown land. They needed help and we were able to provide it.

Meanwhile the Portuguese ministry at Central Baptist continued. I used to knock on doors, talk to people here and there, visit the Portuguese cafés and the local hospital and talk to all those who wanted to hear about the gospel and Central Baptist. I used to go to the Oakville Trafalgar Memorial Hospital to visit Portuguese-speaking people to pray for them at their bedside. They enjoyed these visits, and some would ask me to visit their homes. We had at the church a "call-a-message" telephone; many of them called and some asked me to visit them, which I did.

In the beginning it was only Lucimar, me and the children who would come to church, and we attended the English service. In September of 1987 a couple from Olivet Baptist Church, Paulo and Adriana Rebelo, and their son, Paul Michael, joined us as they lived in Oakville. Together with them we started the Portuguese service in the Anderson Room. After the service we started a Bible study in the office of Rev. Jack Anderson. We were four! In June of 1988 we decided to stop the Portuguese services and the Bible study, and joined the English congregation for the Sunday service, but we continued meeting in our homes and praying for wisdom, guidance and direction regarding the Portuguese ministry. In September we again started the services and the Bible study, with two new families joining us from Brampton. Then another family, Tony and Nelia Martins and their two children, Kelly and Justin, from Mississauga also came to be part of the ministry. It was a great encouragement to us. God was showing me that this was His will for us and Central Baptist Church. He was guiding us.

Baptismal service in the Portuguese ministry, Central Baptist Church, Oakville, Ontario

The ministry requires the missionary to get involved in the Portuguese community, to better know the people and to identify with them in order to share the gospel. It is necessary to demonstrate love, patience and persistence and spend time in prayer. I got involved in the community, trying to understand the people, being the presence of the Kingdom, as Paul said to the church in Corinth, "I have become all things to all people, that I might by all means save some" (1 Corinthians 9:22b). Every week I walked in the Portuguese business area, the supermarket, coffee shops and restaurants. I translated for doctors because many Portuguese people do not speak English. I took some to the Portuguese Alcoholics Anonymous group in Toronto, and then opened a group at Central Baptist, with the support of the Halton Police.

Lucimar was always my support in the ministry, an excellent mother and faithful companion. She also accompanied me in visitation. She was always the volunteer pianist for the Portuguese ministry and organized the choir, the women's association and the Pioneer Club. The Pioneer Club was a blessing in our church. Lucimar felt the need of a program for the Portuguese and English children. It was very important and wonderful to see the children of the Portuguese and English families coming together every Friday for Pioneer Club. It was a marvelous and meaningful time in the church.

At this time the Portuguese ministry was already known in Oakville. Walking on Kerr Street one lady from an office asked me, "What is the difference between your church and my Catholic faith?" She asked me with curiosity wanting to learn about what I was teaching. She continued, giving an example of what she wanted to know. "For example, you don't have images in your churches, but you believe in miracles."

"Maria," I answered, "the difference is only one; we believe in Jesus Christ for our salvation."

"But we also believe."

"Yes, you believe in Jesus," I answered, "but you put beside Jesus the image of a saint and pray to him. The Bible teaches us that we shouldn't add anything to what Jesus did on the cross; He gave His life for us, dying, pouring out His blood to forgive our sins for our salvation."

"Yes, it is true; you are right," she said.

I continued walking, looking for other Portuguese people, on that cold day in a Canadian winter, praying for this community. As I walked, I was thinking about that question posed by Maria, "What is the difference?" How many in the city, on the street where we live and in the family don't know the difference. There are many who still are asking the same question, "What is the difference?" The difference is Jesus Christ, as Luke wrote in his Book of Acts, "There is salvation in no one else, for there is no other name under heaven given among mortals by which we must be saved" (Acts 4:12).

At Easter, Christmas and the church anniversary I wrote a bulletin called *Boas Novas*, which we distributed in the community. During every year that I was a missionary in Oakville we did this work. I was always helped by my two sons Daniel and Marcos. I was very happy that they helped me. Also, people from the congregation helped me, and we sent some through the post office. Sometimes we received some sent back with a note that we should not send any more. Others called the "call-a-message" telephone asking for prayer. One couple not only left a message, but they came to the church and never left. I had the privilege of baptizing Alberto and Fernanda Souza. This couple had lived in Oakville many years and an envelope with a *Boas*

Novas bulletin brought them to accept Christ as their saviour. Praise the Lord!

I did interpretation for the Halton Police probation department. One winter day I went to the house of one of those men for whom I was interpreting. When I arrived at that house, in the garage there were three other people enjoying themselves, each one with a cup of wine in his hand, including the person who was an alcoholic. He was not supposed to drink as he was on probation. Every week he went to the probation officer and I was there to interpret for him.

I started a conversation with them talking about the consequences of drinking and being dependent on alcohol. I had a small empty cross placed on my coat. One of the men approached me and said, "I like this cross," and coming close he touched it and asked, "I very much need a cross like this. It is the cross of our Lord Jesus Christ, isn't it?"

I answered him, "Yes," adding that "Jesus died on the cross, but He is alive; He rose again; He is our saviour."

Then he asked me, "Would you give this cross to me? I need to come closer to Jesus Christ."

I took the cross from my coat and put it on his coat. He was very happy. It was a way to make friends with him and witness about Jesus. There was a soul thirsty for a relationship with Jesus. He gave me his address and I visited and prayed with him, his wife and children many times. At our Good Friday conference, I invited him to come for the service. He and his family came and when the guest speaker, after the sermon, made the appeal for people to accept Christ Manuel was the first to come to the front.

That gathering in that Portuguese house in Oakville was a demonstration of what men do when they are receiving employment insurance during the rigorous Canadian winter. They meet together to converse, to fellowship, and at the same time to make and drink too much wine and become alcoholics.

When I finished my conversation with those men, they all went home, even the owner of the house. He went inside and closed the door. I was left alone at the door, but because I knew him very well, had talked to him many times and interpreted at the Halton Police probation office, I knocked at the door and he opened it. I asked permission to go in. He knew me and let me enter. There he was, drunk, very drunk, lying on a bed. I talked to him for a few minutes while tears were running down his face. I felt very sorry for him, a soul for whom also Jesus had died. This man was in need of salvation that only Jesus can give to change his life. He knew exactly what drinking was doing in his life. I prayed silently and left that house very sad!

Even though we talked about Jesus he couldn't understand that he only needed Jesus Christ and to accept Him by faith. Unfortunately, he always answered me that he would stay where he was, "I was born in this and in this I will die." For a few years I visited that house; he and his wife always treated me very well. One day his wife called me at the church and told me in tears, "Horácio died this morning; he was very drunk." She was very desolate! I went to her home and prayed that God would give her the comfort she needed at that time.

In the summer of 1996, the English and Portuguese ministries distributed a video tape of the movie *Jesus*. This movie, made by Campus Crusade for Christ, depicts the life of Jesus. A team of fourteen Portuguese members of the church went door-to-door giving free copies of the movie to more than one hundred homes. As they knocked on doors some residents would not accept because, they said, they were Catholics. "We are Catholics; we don't want this movie."

However, some accepted it gladly, saw it and liked it. But the response was always, "We do not want to change our religion!"

At the business meeting of the church in October 1997 a motion was introduced to change the support of the Portuguese ministry, which to that date still received financial help from the World Mission Board of the Brazilian Baptist Convention and the Department of Canadian Mission of the Baptist Convention of Ontario and Quebec. In that business meeting a vote passed to change the support of the missionary family. The Portuguese ministry would be the sole responsibility of Central Baptist Church.

Central Baptist Church accepted this decision and created the full-time position of Portuguese Language Pastor. Rev. João Garcia was invited to be the pastor of this ministry. I started in this position on January 1, 1998, even though I continued as a missionary of the World Mission Board of the Brazilian Baptist Convention.

The ministry continued being a presence of the gospel among Portuguese-speaking people. It continued being a local ministry, helping people with all their needs.

Several years we did a retreat at Camp Kwasind. Each October about fifty of us travelled to the camp on Skeleton Lake, Huntsville, Ontario, and spent a weekend studying the Bible, praying and relaxing.

Since coming to Canada, we participated in the Easter Conference that was organized in 1978 by Rev. Dionísio Pape, the pastor of King Street Baptist Church, Preston, Cambridge. He spent many years in Brazil as a missionary of the Canadian Baptist Ministries. Portuguese people come together on Good Friday to celebrate the death, burial and resurrection of Jesus. Every year one church hosts the conference. We have hosted several times. It is a wonderful celebration of the death and resurrection of Jesus and the preaching of the gospel – and also, a great time of fellowship.

After a long time preparing and organizing, we started our home small groups in January of 2002, four groups in Portuguese and five groups in English. The Portuguese ministry had groups in the north and south of Oakville and one in Mississauga. The leaders were chosen and trained by the Portuguese pastor, Rev. João Garcia. Copies of the lessons were distributed to all who came to the small group. It became a great blessing for the spiritual growth of the church. It was also a way of witnessing in the community to the gospel of Jesus Christ.

Every September we celebrated the Portuguese ministry anniversary. Every year we invited a guest speaker from Brazil or Portugal. Although the celebration had the goal of reaching out into the community, it also helped members of the church very much. We came together for the entire weekend, worshiping, praising, praying and visiting the Portuguese community.

A picnic in July was also a part of our summers. We went to Bronte Creek Provincial Park and after a few years we decided to move to Christie Lake Conservation Area. We started at 10 a.m. with a service. It was a time of fellowship, when the families came together and stayed all day enjoying themselves, conversing, some playing soccer and others spending time on the lake.

For many years we had a "call-a-message" in Portuguese. Every week a new message was recorded. Many people called to listen to the message. One day I was at the Portuguese coffee shop when a Portuguese couple waved to me. I went over to see what they wanted. They told me, "For many years we have been listening to the telephone message every week, and it always brings great comfort to our hearts."

After more than twenty years leading the Portuguese ministry at Central Baptist Church in Oakville, the moment of leaving was approaching. I felt that a change in leadership at Central Baptist was imminent. I was over sixty-five years old. Then on July 13, 2007, I presented a letter to the leadership of the church stating that I would retire on November 30, 2007. We were in a way sad but at the same time happy that with love, patience, persistence and prayer we had done Portuguese ministry, following the call of God.

On November 30, the church held a surprise celebration thanking God and Rev. João and Lucimar Garcia for years of ministry in Oakville. Many people were present. It was a very emotional time for us!

We came to Canada – Lucimar, Victor, Daniel and I (Marcos was born in London, Ontario, the first of the Garcia family outside Brazil) – answering the call of God to work among Portuguese people. We started in London, Ontario, where we stayed close to eight years and then we came to Oakville where we stayed more than twenty years. Lucimar helped and supported me in my ministry. She became involved in many areas. Without her support I don't know whether I could have stayed all these years doing this missionary ministry. I give many thanks to God and to her for being beside me all these years. Our children grew up in Canada. They studied, worked and got married and now have their own children. We have five granddaughters and three grandsons, Christian (23), Alyssa (18), Chelsea (11), Hannah (19), Rebekah (17), Marcos (15), Brooklyn (12) and Joshua (8). It is wonderful! We are very happy that they are all around us here in Oakville. We always come together for special events and *Vovô* and *Vovó* (Grandpa and Grandma) are never tired of being with them.

Upon the completion of our work we travelled to Europe for a three-week trip. We visited Switzerland, France, Austria and Germany. In France we visited the city of Kaysersberg, Alsace, and the house where Albert Schweitzer lived. Beside his house is the church where he was the pastor for some time. He left the church and went as a medical missionary to Lambaréné, Gabon, Africa, where he founded the Albert Schweitzer Hospital. In this hospital he treated sick people and at the same time preached the gospel. He developed a philosophy of Reverence for Life. He wrote a book wherein he describes his philosophy (among other books), and he won the Nobel Peace Prize in 1952. We also had an excellent trip around Germany where we visited important places in the life of Luther, from his birth to his death. We travelled to every city where he preached the Reformation of Christianity. After that we went to Austria, where we stayed one week in the Austrian Alps. It was a beautiful trip that we could do only with the help of our cousins Peter and Sylvia Eglin, who live in Basel, Switzerland. We thank them for taking us with them for this strip.

The following year we went to Brazil. In São Paulo we visited Trans World Radio. They organize and publish a periodical of daily devotionals and invited me to be one of their writers, a task that I accepted. The periodical is called *Presente Diário* (Daily Gift). It is volunteer work that I am happy to do, besides preaching in English and Portuguese as I am invited. God always guided me; I was never alone. Praise Him for everything. As Paul said to the church in Philippi, " I have learned this secret, so that anywhere, at any time, I am content" (Philippians 4:12b GNT).

22

SOWING THE WORD

"A sower went out to sow."
– Mark 4:3b

In the Gospel of Mark there is recorded the parable of the sower (Mark 4:1-20). Jesus told this parable to a great multitude that was listening to him on the shore of the Sea of Galilee. Many farmers have had the experience of sowing a seed and watching it spring up into a beautiful plant. In Canada it is wonderful to watch the plants come up after the severe winter and fill the gardens with beautiful flowers. After a severe winter what we plant is born, grows and flourishes. Jesus said in his parable that a sower planted a seed and the result was that it sprouted, grew and gave fruit, "first the stalk, then the head, then the full grain in the head" (Mark 4:28b).

How this happens we don't know. The sowed seed dies in the earth. Paul wrote about this to the church of Corinth, "you do not sow the body that is to be, but a bare seed… But God gives it a body as he has chosen" (1 Corinthians 15:37b-38a). Not even the most experienced farmer can explain how it happens. He knows only that he sows the seed and it sprouts, grows and produces fruit.

During His walks on the dusty roads of Palestine Jesus might have seen many farmers sowing seeds. He must have observed their ways of sowing and their results. And then He used what He had seen to teach His disciples. It was His method of teaching His listeners, using parables. "The kingdom of God is as if someone would scatter seed on the ground" (Mark 4:26). In His parables there is always a central lesson the reader has to learn. Jesus observed the daily life of people and extracted from it lessons for our life; the Kingdom of God was present on earth in His person. The signs, the miracles, His teaching with authority and His power demonstrate the presence of the Kingdom of God; He is here now, and we can understand Him through the lessons of His parables.

Many rejected Him, and, in our day, many still reject Him. In the Portuguese community where I worked for many years, they prefer to pray to the Holy Christ, a wooden image that is kept safe in a chapel in Ponta Delgada, São Miguel, Azores. This image is carried through the streets of the community, once a year, in May. The Portuguese people come out in procession thinking that this image has miraculous power to listen to their prayers. When we visit a Portuguese community, we can see on many doors a tile with the image of *Fátima* or of *Santo Cristo*. The people believe that the tile can protect their homes!

However, Jesus continued patiently sowing the seed of the Kingdom, even though many rejected Him. He knew that others would accept His teaching and follow Him. The sower is, therefore, patient as Jesus was. If we accept the challenge to sow the seed of the Kingdom, we have to be very patient as the sower of the field was, in the hope that eventually we will harvest the fruits of the seeding.

On September 17, 1979, Lucimar, myself and our two older sons, Victor and Daniel, were sent to Canada in a partnership project of the World Mission Board of the Brazilian Baptist Convention with the Department of Canadian Mission of the Baptist Convention of Ontario and Quebec to start a missionary work in London, Ontario, at Adelaide Street Baptist Church, to reach out into the Portuguese community. This church wanted to start a ministry in the community that lived in the area where the church was located, in downtown London, where there were about twenty thousand Portuguese people from the Azores. After some years working among this wonderful people God blessed us and today, we have a Portuguese Baptist Church in London, Ontario, with one hundred and fifty people.[60]

During the time that we spent in London I was informed that there was another city, Strathroy, not far from London that had a large Portuguese community. I went to Strathroy and started walking on the streets looking for people to whom I could talk about the gospel. I walked alone praying, asking God to open a door of a home where I could go in to meet people and witness about Jesus. I spent about five years doing this almost every month. One day a member of the church in London informed me that there was a person in Strathroy that wanted to study the Bible. That was the opportunity that I was looking for.

Immediately I went to Strathroy, now with an address. It was the residence of Frank and Noemia Atayde. When I arrived at the house, I noticed several people in front of the house. They were preparing to go fishing. It was summer and a good time for fishing.

I asked who was called Atayde, and one of them answered, "I am Atayde."

"Pleased to meet you, sir," I said.

"I am pleased, too; you speak Portuguese," he answered and continued, "Who are you?"

I said, "I was informed that you want to study the Bible."

"Yes, but not today. Today I am going fishing with my friends; come back next week."

"*Está bem*! It's okay; I will be back next week."

The following week I started a Bible study in his home. We were always very welcome. They were very happy with our presence. They wanted to know about Jesus, and what the difference is between Catholics and Evangelicals. One snowy and dark night when we arrived at Frank and Noemia's home for our Bible study, as I did not cancel the meeting, we were very surprised the house was packed with other Portuguese couples. They were fishing friends of Atayde. He had invited them to come to listen to the pastor – the "Portuguese Padre," as I was known – who was teaching the Bible.

---

[60] See chapter 19 "On the Banks of the Other Thames River."

When I started the meeting, I asked them to tell me about their religious experience, and I listened carefully. Unfortunately, even though they were Catholics they didn't know too much about what they believed. This has been the methodology that I have followed – listen first with love, with patience and in prayer. In reality these people didn't know the teachings of Jesus. All they knew were the traditions of their church: the pope being the representative of Jesus on earth, having to pray to Mary, baptizing their children, praying before images, purgatory and salvation coming through belonging to the Catholic Church.

I started teaching them that the first thing they had to understand was the authority of Scriptures, that they are the word of God. It is from the Bible that we come to the knowledge of the teachings of Jesus. These wonderful people know the authority of the Catholic Church, their leaders and their traditions, but do not know about the teachings of the Bible. After our study I challenged them to follow only what Jesus taught us; He was the One Who died on the cross, poured out His blood to forgive our sins, was buried and rose again. He is our Saviour. Salvation is not from belonging to the Church. We meet on Sundays as His church to worship Him. That winter night the Holy Spirit convinced those people, seven couples from the Island of São Jorge, Azores, to accept Jesus as their only Saviour.

Some time later, on a Wednesday night, Frank was looking for me in London. He met me at the home of Ernesto and Alda André. I was leading a Bible study with several people from the community. Atayde knocked at the door; Ernesto opened it and Atayde asked, "Is Pastor Garcia here?"

"Yes, he is; come in."

He entered and after saying hello he told all those present in that room, "We want to be baptized, my wife and I and our children, my sister, my son and his wife, my brother Joe and his wife Maria, and probably others."

"Why are you in a hurry?"

"We want to be baptized this Friday, because there is a special flight to the Azores this Saturday, at a very good price, and we want to visit our families there, all of us complete in the faith."

By "complete" they meant that they had accepted Jesus into their lives and wanted to be baptized so they could witness to their families in São Jorge.

The next day I called every member of our church, and fourteen of them were baptized on Friday night after I had interviewed each one of them in my office, before the baptism. It was a night of praising God, happiness and fellowship. It was a wonderful beginning of the new congregation at Strathroy First Baptist Church. Later that church formed a partnership with the Department of Canadian Mission and the Brazilian World Mission Board to bring Rev. Jackson Rondini and his family to Strathroy.

It is impossible to think that a sower throws the seed on the soil believing that it is not going to grow. In the parable in Mark 4:3 Jesus teaches His disciples that "A sower went out to sow." We have the best seed of good quality.

When I was a boy my father had a grocery store where he sold all kinds of fruits, vegetables, plants and seeds. Sometimes I observed the people who came to buy seeds, and usually they asked my father, "Mr. Manoel, are the seeds of good quality?"

He always answered, "Of course!"

My father would never sell seeds that were not of good quality, though they needed to be sowed to produce good fruits. That is precisely what Jesus is teaching us, that the good seed, the word of God, needs to be sowed. The sower sows the seed of the best quality.

It is exactly what we are doing as missionaries in Oakville, after spending almost eight years in London, Ontario. When we moved to Oakville, we had no idea what the town was like. We knew only where the church was located. When we started the ministry, we were intimidated by the wealth of the town. It was a great challenge! The question that I had in my mind was how to do the work in such a church and such a town, how to go to this people so rooted in their traditions.

But God, Who knows that missionaries walk by faith, went with us and opened doors so I could go in and explain the gospel. I became a member of the Halton Multicultural Council, to help new immigrants to Canada; I went to the hospital to visit patients who spoke Portuguese; I helped with translating for the Halton Police; I took people to Toronto Western Hospital every week for the Alcoholics Anonymous program; I translated in the Catholic schools, for Portuguese parents who didn't speak English. God was showing me that inside those beautiful houses there are people in need of knowing the message of Jesus Christ to change their lives.

One sunny afternoon I knocked at the door of a house, but there was no answer. I knocked again and a voice, lonely and painful, now answered, "Come through here." That voice was coming from the basement and again I heard that whispered voice saying, "You can come in; I am here, downstairs."

I went down the stairs and found, in front of me, a large room and in one corner a bed, where someone was lying down. He was covered by a blanket even though it was summer. When he saw me, he said with tears running down his face, "Nobody has ever visited me, except my parents," and he continued, saying, "Everybody is afraid of this scary disease."

I had never seen that young man before; I didn't know him or his parents. He was very touched by my visit. I looked for a chair, sat in front of him and told him why I was there that afternoon.

"I am here because Jesus sent me to you! He has the power to give you the relief you need."

Then I prayed for him. God is compassionate and merciful. Psalm 78 tells us that the people of Israel rebelled against Him, abandoned Him and did things that He didn't approve, but, nevertheless, instead of sending judgement, God "remembered that they were but flesh, a wind that passes and does not come again" (Psalm 78:39). He then showed mercy to them and being a compassionate God "forgave their iniquity, and did not destroy them" (Psalm 78:38), forgave them as He forgives us today, those who come close to Him, in any circumstances of life.

I went out of that house with tears in my eyes, seeing what the devil does in the lives of those who do not belong to God. I continued my walk in the community always praying for that young man and many others who are far from God. A few days later I went back to visit him again, but I didn't find him; he had died after my last visit.

This is the task of the sower. "A sower went out to sow" (Mark 4:3). He sowed with patience. His faith is shown in his patience. Once he sows, he cannot do anything more. It is not up to him to make the seed grow. He will be a fool if he goes out at dawn and digs the soil to check whether or not the seed is growing. As the mere human beings we are, we have this tendency. We become inpatient. We want to know what is happening with seed that we sowed. But the sower of the parable went home after sowing and waited until the seed germinated and grew, "yielding thirty and sixty and a hundredfold" (Mark 4:8b).

Every week I went out to talk to Portuguese people. One day I met this man from the Island of São Jorge. He said, "Come to my home." I went and I was welcomed by him and his wife. They were very happy I was there to visit them. They offered me coffee and we started talking about Brazil, the Azores and the difference between their church and ours.

After our visit I left praying for that couple, that they might understand that we need only Jesus for our spiritual life. The traditions of the church do not help us to find salvation. I went back to that house and gave them a Portuguese Bible. I did not know that they were planning to go back to the Island of São Jorge. They went back taking their youngest son. The Bible was forgotten inside of their luggage!

When they were living on the Island of São Jorge, their son found the Bible and started reading it. He asked permission from his father to go to the local evangelical congregation for the Sunday service. He went for the first time on a Sunday morning. That church was a small congregation, the result of missionary work. The young man liked it so much that he continued going back, and never left. He also started studying his Bible; being taught by the missionary he accepted Jesus and was baptized.

After a few years he felt the call to the ministry, went to the seminary and became the pastor of that small congregation on the Island of São Jorge. He felt the need to come back to Canada to witness to his family who live here in Oakville about what God had done in his life. He came to Central Baptist Church, brought all his relatives, some of whom I knew, and gave his testimony here in the pulpit of the Portuguese ministry. Today he is the pastor, together with his wife and children, at an evangelical church in Algarve, Portugal.

In my visits to the Oakville hospital I met a patient with whom I spoke for some time. When he left the hospital, I went to see him at his home where I met his wife. They came from the Island of São Jorge. I invited them to come to church to worship God in Portuguese. It took some time, but one Sunday they came. After the service I spoke to them and they said, "We liked the Mass," and since then they have been coming every Sunday.

The seed was sowed in their hearts. Ten years had passed and one Wednesday morning they came to my office and both of them said, "We came here today to ask you to baptize us." I had the privilege of baptizing them at the Sunday morning service. They were very happy and so was the whole Portuguese congregation. Praise God!

After a Sunday morning service, a woman member of our congregation asked me, "Pastor, can you visit my sister-in-law?"

"Yes, of course," I answered.

"Would you be able to go this week?"

"I will call you and let you know the day."

Lucimar and I were very surprised when we arrived at the house. It was a very small basement apartment. The young woman was living there with her four children. Ten years before, she had arrived in Canada as an emigrant from the Island of São Miguel, with the hope of a better life for them. At that time, they had only two children.

A few years later that young woman had a great disappointment; her husband left her. She was left with two children, sad, lonely and frightened. What was she to do in a strange land and with no knowledge of English? She looked for a job and found one cleaning offices at night. She left her two children with a family that was willing to help her. At her work she talked to a man who asked her to read Psalm 34:18, where it says that God is always close to us, "The LORD is near to the brokenhearted."

She went home and read the Psalm, which touched her life, but she was not yet ready to give her life to Jesus. She was Catholic and would stay in her church, although it had been a long time since she had gone to Mass. Unfortunately, there are many people who think that saying "I am a Christian" is enough. They never go regularly to worship God. However, the gospel teaches us that it is necessary to give our lives to Jesus and follow Him. That young woman came to understand this a few years later.

At the same place where she worked, she met a man who made thousands of promises to her. She believed him and as a result she had two more sons. That person lied to her, left her and went back to his own country. Now she was alone again and with four children. That was when she went to live in this small basement apartment; it was all the rent that she could pay.

When Lucimar and I arrived at that basement she was very sad. We started talking to her about Jesus, why He came into this world, His life, His teaching and His love for each one of us. We told her that God knows that we are mere human beings. He is compassionate, forgives, heals our wounds and works wonders when we give our lives to Him and trust in Him. We mentioned to her a hymn that we sing in our services, "Trust in God that He always will listen to you." That day Lucimar and I prayed for her, her children and also for her husband wherever he was. We asked God to touch his heart and that one day he might come back home. This, however, from a human point of view was an impossibility, but not for God if she would trust in Him.

From that day on she started coming to our Portuguese services. She also came for the Friday prayer meetings, when we also had a children's program. Her four children enjoyed going to Pioneer Club.

One night after our prayer meeting, I went to my office. It was about ten o'clock in the evening. I was getting ready to turn off the light and go home when someone knocked at the door. I opened the door quite surprised as no one usually goes to my office at that time. It was a young man whom I had never seen before. He immediately said, "I know that my wife is coming to this church, because my sister told me. I am her husband," and he continued, saying, "I also want to follow the Jesus that she is following. I know that only He can help me."

That young husband came back home. It was a very difficult process of re-adaptation, learning to accept living with two other children that were not his. He had to learn to live a new life, but Jesus always can help, and can make all things new. Instead of bringing judgement He forgives. He is compassionate; He is merciful. He forgave that young husband and taught him to accept those two wonderful children, who today are grown up. Paul wrote in his second letter to the church in Corinth "everything old has passed away; see, everything has become new!" (2 Corinthians 5:17b) I had the great privilege of baptizing the whole family. Now when they come on Fridays for the prayer meeting, we can hear that young husband praying with such emotion that it touches all of us at the meeting. "Ah, my Lord, thank you! What a marvelous thing you have done in my life; praise your name! You have taken me from that terrible life I was living, brought me back home and gave me salvation and now I live a happy life together with my family."

One married woman came to our house, knocked on the front door, came in and sat on the couch; desperate and with tears she said, "Pastor and Lucimar, I don't know what to do in life; my husband doesn't change; he is destroying our home."

After listening to the lament of that woman, we prayed together for God to work a miracle in their lives. I told her before she left our house that God has the power to change people. He can change your lament into a song of joy. "We will continue praying for you and your husband," I said to her.

God changed the life of her husband. It was a long walk of faith, patience and hope, without any doubt. He became sober and a follower of Jesus. He was well known and loved in the community with the nick name "rotten." But when he came to Jesus his nick name was changed to "recovered." I had the privilege of baptizing that couple. Now in his house there is a poster with the words of Paul in his letter to the Romans, "If God is for us, who is against us?" (Romans 8:31b) Not even the power of the devil can be against those who belongs to Jesus; "everything old has passed away" (2 Corinthians 5:17b).

The sower is called to sow. He sows with love, patience, persistence and prayer. The harvest belongs to God; it will come in His time. We don't know how this happens, but the seed that was sown will produce in God's time. He opened the waters of the red sea; He guided His people through the dry land of the desert; He led His people as a flock. He does the same with His people today. The seed sprouted in the hearts of those who have accepted Jesus. Now they belong to the Kingdom. Therefore, there is no doubt that our God will guide us as a flock in the vagaries of our lives. The seed was sown with faith; it germinated, grew and produced as we faithfully waited on Him.

MISSION IN THE AZORES

"Azores, a freshness and a special charm"
– Carreiro da Costa[61]

We arrived in the Azores for a three-week missionary visit. We were very happy with this great opportunity to share the gospel with the Azorean people. After fourteen years of missionary work among Portuguese people in Canada we now were coming to visit the islands where most of them were from, looking for a better life for the family.

Ponta Delgada, São Miguel Island, is a great and beautiful city. It looks like any city in Europe. Houses of antique construction told us a little about the history of Portugal. It was the Portuguese who populated the nine islands of the Azores. This means that when the Portuguese navigators, working for the king of Portugal, arrived on these islands there were no people living there, unlike the case of Brazil and Angola, where they found a population of native people.

---

[61] Francisco Carreiro da Costa, *Etnologia dos Açores*, Lagoa, 1989, p. 273.

It was a surprise to see big islands, beautiful cities, progress and a better understanding of the Portuguese history. Of course, on the Island of Terceira, I had to be careful when I spoke to people about my Spanish roots. History tells us that it was on Terceira that the Spanish soldiers were expelled when they tried to conquer the island. A legend says that they were frightened by a country girl, Brianda Pereira, who, with the help of the local priest, drove a thousand fierce bulls at the totally unaware poor Spanish soldiers![62] They ran for their lives! The Battle of Salga is still remembered with laughter and as a joke, especially when a Spaniard is visiting Terceira!

Faial is another beautiful island. Porto Pim is a place for yachts and boats to stop for a while on their journey from Europe to America. For some this stop takes about a week as they discover how interesting that island is. A couple from Holland told me with an expression of amazement, "This is a marvelous island."

The Azoreans are a very religious people, following the Roman Catholic traditions. They built very beautiful churches all around the islands. In the countryside the *impérios* are built in the same style as the churches. They are part of the cult of the Empire of the Holy Spirit. In Portuguese it is called *Culto do Império do Espírito Santo*. "It is a religious sub-culture, inspired by Christian millenarian mystics, associated with Azorean Catholic identity…"[63] It involves traditional and religious celebration in the countryside communities of the Azores, dedicated to the Divine Holy Spirit.

The Portuguese writer João E. C. Leite in his book *Estrangeiros nos Açores* (Foreigners in the Azores) mentions the cult of the Holy Spirit. He says this:

"Among the amusements of the countryside people, there is the cult of the Holy Spirit, which is celebrated in every parish, for seven weeks. Every Sunday, during the sung Mass, the priest puts a silver crown on the head and a scepter in the hand of a peasant, previously selected by the people. He is proclaimed emperor… On the seventh and last Sunday of the celebration of the cult of the Holy

---

[62] July 25, 1581.

[63] *Wikipedia*, under the words "Cult of the Holy Spirit." See the "History" section about when and by whom it was started.

Spirit, in the morning, the emperor sits in the *império*[64] and in front of him a table is set with bread and wine, and two or three of his closest friends sit to the right and left. The emperor stays in this place until night.

"During all this time the faithful take bread, wine and meat to be blessed. Some of the food on the table is shared and the rest is distributed to the poor. The same day, the people select the emperor for the following year, to whom the crown and the scepter are given to take home and put in a room that is prepared for this purpose and stay there until next year."[65]

A convent in Ponta Delgada, São Miguel Island, keeps the image of the *Santo Cristo*. It is an old image of Christ venerated by all Azorean people. I tried to see it, but a sister who came to help us told us that the image can be seen by the public only once a year, when a great celebration takes place, with pilgrims from all over the world coming to participate in it. It is taken in a procession through the streets of Ponta Delgada and all the people are required to follow along.

There are some people who do not participate in this procession. They are the evangelicals who follow only Jesus Christ and do not accept this type of idolatry. In Ponta Delgada there are several evangelical churches. At our first service at the local Baptist church a wonderful group of people came to listen to the word of God. When we were praying a group of children prayed too, giving thanks for the salvation they received from Jesus Christ.

After this service we were taken to a small village, Lomba de São Pedro, where there is a Presbyterian church. From this village many emigrated to London, Ontario. That night we felt the presence of God very much in our midst, in the tent that was raised for the purpose of having an evangelistic service. Several people responded to the appeal that was made at the end of the service.

Dr. Roger, a medical doctor at the hospital in Ponta Delgada, and Dr. Joed Venturine told us about the difficulties of being

---

[64] An *império* (meaning "empire") is a small structure, with a distinct architectural style, where the faithful conduct their rituals.

[65] João E. C. Leite, *Estrangeiros nos Açores*, p. 178-179.

evangelical medical doctors in a Roman Catholic tradition. Many times, they are the object of laughter and jokes.

On a Monday night we were teaching a text from the Bible and one man, who was present at that house, was looking at me as though he had never listened to the gospel. I was explaining what Jesus meant when He said, "Come to me" (Matthew 11:28a). These people have been taught that they have to go to Mary and pray for her help, but Jesus said to go to Him, not to Mary!

On the Island of Faial, the World Mission Board of the Brazilian Baptist Convention supports a missionary and his family, who are doing an excellent mission. Several people have accepted Jesus Christ as their saviour and are coming to the services every Sunday. On Terceira Rev. Tiago Pereira is the pastor of two congregations at Praia da Vitória and Angra do Heroismo; God has used this brother in the development of those churches. When I preached in those churches the sanctuary was packed. The possibilities are many, but the mission on these islands is not easy. It takes a long time until someone understands who Jesus really was, and why He came into this world.

As missionaries we are called here in Canada, in the Azores or anywhere in the world to witness that only Jesus has the power to give us a life of intimacy with God, because He died on the cross pouring out His blood for our salvation. The Baptist churches in the Azores are part of our family, a faithful remnant. We thank God for the opportunity He gave us, Lucimar and me, to visit and preach in those churches.

24

&

MISSION IN CUBA:
Christianity Is Not an Idea

"It is no longer I who live, but it is Christ who lives in me."
– Paul in Galatians 2:20

    I was going back to Cuba once more. On that same Cubana Airlines flight was also travelling a group of young people from Dante Alighieri Academy in Toronto. They were very happy to visit Havana, unconcerned with the situation in Cuba. I was praying that God would guide and prepare me for my mission to meet with more than a hundred young mem who were working as missionaries in several cities in Cuba. The Brazilian World Mission Board supports them, and I was going to supervise their work.

    As soon as I arrived at the Havana airport the customs officer asked me what I was going to do in Cuba.

    "I am a religious person and I am going to visit churches," I answered.

    "You can't preach in Cuba; if you want to, you have to go to the immigration office in Havana to get a religious visa that gives you permission to preach."

I left customs, took my luggage, met Rev. Nilo Dominguez and told him what the officer had said. In his very old car, we went to his home. He then, expressing no surprise, said, "Ah, these men! They want more currency, more money," and he continued, "Don't worry; everything is okay."

He showed me my usual place, a bed in the sitting room, close to the window, from where I could see the backyard with lots of orange trees and also the building of the Baptist church. In Cuba it's always sunny! It was very hot. So, I went outside to relax under the shade of an orange tree. There I met a young man who was also enjoying the shade, waiting for the choir rehearsal to start. We introduced ourselves and started a conversation.

He was very happy to meet me and, because I was a pastor, he told me about an episode in his life, when he was arrested for being a teacher in the Sunday school of his church.

"When I was twelve years old, my father started teaching me about what was going on in Cuba. We were living in the sixties, and Fidel Castro was already in power. My father told me that El Comandante was a communist. And then he continued, telling me that I should be very careful because being a Christian I could be put in jail if I continued going to church. That was exactly what happened one Sunday after the morning service. That day I had taught the children's Sunday school class. That was not allowed. The revolution soldiers took me – I was then twenty-two years old – ten years after my father had warned me about the communist revolution. They put me into a truck together with other Christians and took us to a jail. From there, every day they took us to cut sugar cane. I stayed in prison two years and did not die because of my Christian behaviour. God was faithful and protected me as I never left Him. I worked from dawn to dusk, doing hard work, with little food, but I survived; since I went back home, to this day, I continue serving God, with my family and in my church."

Today the situation is not as bad. They do not put pastors in prison, don't close churches and do not forbid Christians to go to church and to evangelize. Today there is another tactic to achieve their ultimate goal, to stop Christianity from growing. It is the method that El Comandante, Fidel Castro, called the "Battle of Ideas" as he believed that today debating ideas is more important than persecuting Christians and their churches.

A Christian brother told me what El Comandante said: "We have to work with ideas and put these ideas into the population, starting in the schools, teaching children and young people what Che Guevara and El Comandante Fidel Castro teach, that *patria* (mother country) is the most important. The country is formed of new men without corruption or personal ambition and not working for self but for the country. The new man is one whom the world should see and admire and desire to be like, as in our country. The new man thinks of a classless society where everything is common to all."

What they do today is to compete with the church, trying to teach these ideas to the children. The police in Cuba no longer persecute the churches, or destroy them, but compete with them. "We will tell the children that Christianity is no longer important but rather the community." So, they started a program every Sunday in the schools, at the same time as the church Sunday school. They insist that all children should go to that school instead of the church Sunday school.

The authorities in Cuba do not understand that Christianity is not an idea. Christian life is not an idea that we discuss and that can be replaced by another, but it is a relationship, a daily life with a person, Jesus Christ. And this person did not come into this world to preach an idea, a philosophy or a pedagogical theory. Jesus came to preach that all people are sinners, but they can be forgiven and enter the Kingdom of God through Him. It is His blood poured out on the cross that enables us to have a relationship with God; "the blood of Jesus his Son cleanses us from all sin" (1 John 1:7b). And when we accept the sacrifice of Jesus on the cross, we have the assurance of a better life here and in eternity. That is why the Christian children who are in the state school say without any fear, as a brave ten-year-old girl said to her teacher, "Teacher, Sunday is the day to go to church. I don't come to the celebration in the school because I am going to the Sunday school in my church."

Finishing my work in Havana I flew to Santiago de Cuba, and from there, with Pastor Roy Acosta and the driver Ebenezer, in a 1984 Toyota, we travelled to Baracoa. It was a trip of about three hundred kilometres along a narrow highway that has 261 curves and a beautiful view of the Caribbean Sea, the mountains, and plantations of bananas, coffee and cocoa.

The Italian navigator, Christopher Columbus, under the auspices of the Catholic monarchs of Castile and Aragon, docked at a place called Porto Santo in 1492. In 1511 Diego Velázquez de Cuéllar was named the first governor of Cuba and founded a settlement which he called Our Lady of the Assumption (known by the natives as Baracoa). This village was the first capital of Cuba. In our day this town is visited by many tourists. It is the poorest region of Cuba, but it is also where there are the most numbers of Christians. Fifteen per cent of the population belong to an evangelical church.

In these mountains, in Guantánamo Province, there are several missionaries supported by the World Mission Board of the Brazilian Baptist Convention. I met with eight of them at the Baracoa Second Baptist Church to listen to their report about the work they are doing. We had an excellent meeting, praying for the mission that they are doing in this beautiful region of Cuba.

It is a very difficult mission as transportation is precarious. The missionaries do not have bicycles; they have to walk long distances to arrive at the place where a meeting has been scheduled. Nevertheless, the message of the gospel has been preached.

In our meeting at the Baracoa Second Baptist Church I asked the missionaries to present their report and also to tell us how they arrived at that meeting. Some live as if hidden in those mountains!

"Pastor Garcia, I walked to the house of this brother (pointing to another missionary) and with him we came by tricycle."

"Pastor, I came by mule to the house of my friend and from there we walked together. The mule is at my friend's house."

"Pastor, I came by bicycle."

None of them came by car for they do not have cars!

We continued our meeting and I asked them to enumerate the challenges they encounter doing the work in that region. They all agreed that there are four things very difficult to deal with:

1. Macumba / Voodoo – There are a lot of people pursuing this African religion, for they think that voodoo will give them a better life.
2. Alcoholism – Every weekend the government sells very cheap rum. People go to a truck that is parked in a given place where they buy it and become drunk.
3. Poverty – People are afraid of losing what they have. If they become Christians, they cannot be members of the Communist

Party; so, they are afraid of loosing what the government gives to them.
4. Politics – There is a battle of ideas, pressure to belong to the Communist Party.

We drove back to Santiago de Cuba where I visited and preached in three churches. In one of them the congregation meets under a tree, where there are benches protected by a fence to keep out the chickens and to make it their own place. On those benches, under a tree, eight of us had our meeting discussing the program for the mission in that area of Santiago de Cuba. There I heard their reports. One of them told us, "It is marvelous to see the results of our work; lately we have had several people coming to Christ." After the meeting this missionary took me to the church where we saw a few pictures showing people being baptized. What is happening in Cuba is that people are meeting in small groups during the week.

In spite of all the difficulties, the church in Cuba is growing, growing because Christians are witnessing that Jesus is not an idea, but a person Who came into the world to reveal God. He became a man, lived among us, died on a cross, poured out His blood, was buried, rose, ascended to heaven, is at the right hand of God, intercedes for us and will come back again. (Philippians 2:5-11)

APPENDIX

25

HERITAGE FROM THE LORD

"Sons are indeed a heritage from the LORD,
the fruit of the womb a reward."
– Psalm 127:3

God gave to Lucimar and me three wonderful sons, Victor Manoel, Daniel Conrado and Marcos Raphael. They are our joy and crown. We walk together as a family richly blessed. We have learned through the years the secret of being content as Paul wrote in his letter to the Philippians (Philippians 4:12b GNT). In moments of happiness or sadness, problems or difficulties in life, we always came together to look for God. He always listens to our prayers.

On March 26, 1974, at the Santa Brigida Maternity Hospital, 1705 Guilherme Pugsley Street, Água Verde, Curitiba, Paraná, Brazil, our first son, **Victor Manoel**, was born. His name is a combination of the names of Lucimar's father and my father, two family and religious men who worked very hard to give the best to their children.

In his first year of life Victor had serious health problems, but by the grace of God and with treatment he was completely healed. He lived five years with us in Curitiba and Ponta Grossa before we came to Canada. His grandma Elvira, Lucimar's mother, was delighted with her first grandchild and so was his grandfather Victor, who called him *Manezinho* (little Manoel).

Every time we travelled to Avaré, the city where Lucimar was born and where her parents and grandparents lived, as soon as we arrived grandma Dorothea took him and Daniel to pick some little fruits in the backyard garden, where she cultivated several different delicious berries, vegetables and legumes; it was a joyful fiesta! The time passed by too fast for Lucimar because of our overseas missionary call to somewhere far away from all our families. We missed the interactions with our family in Brazil.

When we arrived in Canada we went to live in London, Ontario, to work at Adelaide Street Baptist Church as missionaries of the Department of Canadian Mission of the Baptist Convention of Ontario and Quebec and the World Mission Board of the Brazilian Baptist Convention. At first, we stayed with Mr. Roy Taylor and Mae Taylor for about a month until we found a house to rent in Byron, a very nice subdivision in London. At the Taylors' we were introduced to life in Canada. They became like adopted parents and grandparents to our children as we did not have any family in this cold land of Canada.

Appendix

Victor started elementary school at Byron Southwood Public School. There he started leaning the English language. At first, he had some difficulties in understanding everything that was going on as he was only five years old and did not know the English language. He was having a cultural shock. Once, I was called to the school and, when I arrived, he was crying. He needed to go to the washroom, and he did not know how to say it in English. I explained to the teacher what was happening, and she very kindly gave him a hug and took him to the washroom. That was a traumatic experience for him. He continued in that school as we moved to another subdivision in London. He then was transferred to Tweedsmuir Public School, where he also had a wonderful time and a few friends.

He was always very active in the church and paid attention to his father's preaching. When he was ten years old, he was baptized by immersion at the newly organized London Portuguese Baptist Church, 501 Nelson Street, in London, Ontario.

After eight years in London we went to Brazil before moving to our next missionary field. We lived there five months in a city called Campinas, close to São Paulo. In the apartment building where we lived Victor started showing his gift of leadership, teaching the children who also lived in that building to play hockey, the favourite sport of Canada. It was a great novelty at that time for the Brazilian boys who are aficionados of soccer, the national sport. It was, however, difficult to teach hockey to the boys as there were no hockey sticks, not even for sale in the stores! Then an improvisation came along – Victor and Daniel started using brooms as hockey sticks. Every day they played in the parking lot of the apartment building.

When we came back from Brazil we went to live temporarily in Hamilton, Ontario, where Victor, Daniel and Marcos went to public school. Five months later we moved to Oakville, where they were registered at Eastview Public School, on Hixon Street, where they stayed until grade eight and then moved to T. A. Blakelock High School. After high school Victor went to Fanshawe College, London, Ontario, for journalism.

In his last year of high school, Victor went to a business conference in Montreal, where he met a young lady, Linda Moretto. They became friends and she moved to London; they became engaged and I had the privilege of marrying them at Central Baptist Church.

From this marriage two beautiful children were born, Christian Emmanuel and Alyssa Faith. Christian, as a teenager, was a good hockey goalie. Now he is working and learning to be a millwright technician. Alyssa is a beautiful girl, talented and a natural leader. She is always organizing and leading at school or at home. She is now eighteen, taking a course in criminal law at Mohawk College as she wants to proceed to studying at university to be a lawyer.

A few years later, after separation from Linda, Victor met Ashley Noble, a lovely young lady. From this marriage a beautiful girl was born, Chelsea Grace. She is now eleven years old and makes us all happy.

Victor is involved in his church, The Meeting House, where he belongs to a home church with Bible study and prayer. He also is very active in helping refugees. We give thanks to God for his life.

In September 1975, we moved to Ponta Grossa, a city one hundred kilometres west of Curitiba, in the State of Paraná, Brazil, where I went to be the senior pastor of First Baptist, a large church with six hundred fifty members. On May 2, 1976, our second son, **Daniel Conrado**, was born at the Santana Maternity Hospital, 750 Paula Xavier Street. He was very cute! All the family liked him and were very proud of him. One lady from the church, Dona Lula, was always carrying him everywhere, and also Victor. From childhood he was the "engineer" of the family as he enjoyed taking his toys apart and then putting them back together!

His first school, in London, Ontario, was E. D. Roosevelt Public School, 560 Second Street. There he first learned the letters of the alphabet. From that school he went to Tweedsmuir Public School.

When we lived in Campinas for a short time, he also taught some Brazilian children to play hockey. He enjoyed going to a soccer game, and in Campinas we went several times to watch the Guarani play against other clubs from São Paulo. It was a thrill, but a big challenge to get tickets! It was total disorganization, hundreds of people trying to buy entrance tickets at the same time at only one small window in the stadium; nevertheless, we always got them! We were happy and enjoyed being part of the crowd watching those games together.

He was a soccer player for the school and the town of Oakville. He played for the Eastview Public School, on Hixon Street, and for Blakelock High School, on Rebecca Street, Oakville.

Daniel was always determined and was attracted to great adventures. Only after his wedding was it that Lucimar and I came to know of some of his feats, such as parachute jumping, bungee jumping and other sports that require courage, determination and adventure.

Finishing high school, Daniel was accepted at Seneca College for the Computer Engineering Course. He lived close to the college, shared an apartment with his best friend, Rodney, and every weekend came to visit us. When he finished his course at Seneca, he transferred to McMaster University, obtained a BA in Psychology and continued studying, taking the Master of Theology program at McMaster Divinity College.

He was always involved in youth ministry and home church and, at The Meeting House, was also an elder. At a retreat of our church he met a beautiful young lady, Christine Bayley-Mead, and I married them at Central Baptist Church, Oakville. They had three beautiful children, Hannah Isabel, Rebekah Ruth and Marcos Richard (*Marquinhos*). They all participated in church programs. Hannah went on a short mission to the Dominican Republic, where her World Vision group helped to build a small house for a family. Rebekah is a leader and is a teacher in The Meeting House Sunday school. She also travelled with World Vision to China, where their group helped in a social project. Marcos, or *Marquinhos* (little Marcos) as we call him, is a very clever boy. He played soccer and lately plays volleyball on the high school team and also for the town of Oakville. He is a very dedicated student.

On November 30, 1980, our third son was born, here in Canada, at St. Joseph's Hospital, London, Ontario. We called him **Marcos Raphael**; he was born strong, and very healthy. But as days passed Lucimar became very worried because Marcos didn't like eating. We took him to a pediatrician, who told us that he should be alone with food in front of him. "He will eat as he likes," said the doctor. He would play with the food, throw food on the floor and sometimes eat a little. He was a very happy baby! It was at this time that Lucimar was helped by a wonderful "Canadian grandma," Mae

Taylor, who was always ready to assist, as she had a gift to serve. She was the adopted grandma. We had no family in Canada; Roy and Mae Taylor helped with the three boys as we needed. They also loved our children and were always giving gifts to them. To this day we give thanks to God for preparing such a wonderful and caring couple in Canada, when we most needed them. Up to this day the children call them Grandma and Grandpa.

Marcos was four months old when we decided to go for a trip to Louisville, Kentucky, to visit the Southern Baptist Theological Seminary where Dr. Lewis Drummond was a professor. He was my professor at Spurgeon's College, London, England, when he was writing his book about Charles Spurgeon, *Prince of Preachers*. Before we travelled, a wonderful Portuguese couple who belonged to our church in London, Mr. and Mrs. Josué and Inês da Silva, insisted that we leave Marcos with them during our trip. As we never could say "no" we left him with them. We went on our trip and when we came back, we learned that there had been an accident involving them and Marcos, which I describe in chapter 19 "On the Banks of the Other Thames River," page 150.

Marcos started elementary school when we were living in Pond Mills, London. He was registered at Tweedsmuir Public School. Every day he went together with Victor and Daniel in the school bus that picked them up at Glen Roy Crescent. He was always very happy to go with them and all the children of the subdivision.

In June 1983, we went back to Brazil for four months, to visit the family and also because I had to work with the World Mission Board, preaching in many churches and talking about the missionary work in Canada. It was at this time that the family met for the first time the Canadian Marcos Garcia. He also was very excited about meeting the Garcia and Calvello families. He is the first of both families to be born outside Brazil. There was a big party when we arrived at the house of Grandpa and Grandma in Avaré and also at the house of Uncle Euclides and Aunt Tatá in Ponta Grossa, where my mother was living.

We returned to Canada and he continued studying at Tweedsmuir. When we lived for a while in Hamilton, he went to school and, when we moved to Oakville, he went to Eastview Public School, where he stayed until grade eight. Then he went to Blakelock High School. He applied and was accepted at Mohawk College into the Economics Course, which was not for him. He then tried to be a chef and also a tool and die maker, but he was not happy with either. Then he decided to travel and drove to Kamloops, British Colombia, where he had some friends. He stayed there for a while and returned to Oakville, Ontario. He needed a permanent job, and I introduced him to a member of the Portuguese congregation who is the owner of a carpentry company. Silas Almeida accepted him and taught him the profession that he has to this day. Marcos is a great worker and now has his own contract renovation company. Silas told me once that he had never met a young man who learned as quickly as Marcos. He is a very good worker, careful and honest.

Here in Oakville he met a beautiful and wonderful girl, Kathryn Elizabeth Walsh, whom he married on July 30, 2006. They had two beautiful children, Brooklyn and Joshua John Douglas, who make us very happy. They are very active, funny and dramatic! They both go to a Catholic school where they are learning religious lessons, mainly about the Bible. When we are at the table Josh likes to pray before dinner. Brooklyn likes to write stories and shows an ability to make videos on the computer; she surprises us with her creativity.

Lucimar and I give thanks to our God every day for these three wonderful sons He has have given to us, for our daughters-in-law and for our beautiful grandchildren who bring us so much happiness and joy. They are a great blessing. What would have become of us if we had not received this blessed inheritance?

26

&

JETE, GRANADA, SPAIN

"The dawn in the sky greets the day with a sigh for Granada"
– Augustin Lara

Lucimar and I went to Spain with Rev. Jack Anderson and Lois Anderson in May 2011. We stayed at a tourist resort in Marbella, in southern Spain's Costa del Sol. One Monday morning we decided to visit the town of Jete, in the province of Granada, where my father was born. We arrived at Almuñécar, a town on Spain's south Costa Tropical, in the province of Granada, about 12 noon. We found a good restaurant at the entrance of town. I parked the car, and, before entering the restaurant, I crossed the street and went into a small grocery store to ask for directions to Jete. We were close to the town, but I didn't know which street would take me there. The lady in the grocery store, in a very wonderful Spanish tongue, kindly explained that downtown I should take the road called El Suspiro del Moro, which leads to Jete.

A legend says that when the Moors (Muslims) were finally conquered by the Catholic monarchs King Ferdinand II of Aragon and Queen Isabella I of Castile, in 1492, and expelled from Granada, the last Moorish ruler, Sultan Boabdil, King of Al-Andalus, stopped for a while in the southern Sierra Nevada and in that moment sighed deeply as he looked, into the distance, at the palaces he had left in Granada, especially the Alhambra. His mother, who was with him, showed her anger and shame that Boabdil had refused to fight, and spoke the famous phrase recorded in the history of Spain, "Weep like a woman for what you could not defend like a man." Since then, that road is known as El Suspiro del Moro (the Arab's Sigh).

I went back to the restaurant where Lucimar, Jack and Lois were already sitting at a table covered with a blue cloth. We savoured a Mediterranean soup, accompanied with a very good Spanish wine. As soon as we finished our lunch, we continued our trip to Jete. We took El Suspiro del Moro road, winding through the Sierra Nevada, on the tropical coast of Andalucía. Going up we could see the beauty of the region, and rich plantations. Sometimes in my mind I would ask myself why my grandparents and my parents left that land to venture to a distant country in South America.

About one hour into our journey we arrived at the entrance of a small town. A sign beside a plantation of loquats indicated that we were arriving at Jete – *Bienvenido a Jete* (Welcome to Jete). I stopped the car for a while, crossed the road, took a picture, picked up a loquat, returned to the car and drove to the town, located south of Granada. I parked the car in front of the town hall, climbed a long and beautiful set of stairs to a room where the mayor of the town was helping people who came with different questions. His secretary was having lunch and a siesta.

Kindly he asked me, "Can I help you?"

"I am from Brazil," I said, "and I would like to know whether my father had been registered in the registry office?"

"Do you have his birth date?"

"Yes," I answered, "here it is – January 29, 1899."

He took a book off the shelf for the year 1899, and turned several pages until he found it and showed me. "Here it is, Manoel Fernandes Pretel was born in this town and registered in this registry office."

He then made a copy, signed it and gave it to me. He didn't charge, said goodbye and was about to leave, as his secretary was just arriving for the afternoon shift. But, before he left, I asked him why so many people in the past left Spain for South America. He looked at me intently and said, "At the beginning of the last century there was not too much work in this country; therefore, many people had no money and no food. Some were starving and thousands of Spaniards decided to emigrate to Brazil and Argentina. The news from Brazil was that there was lots of work in coffee plantations."

Jete is located in a valley in the Sierra Nevada. I went down alone by the stairs that takes one to the low side of the town. I walked through the narrow streets with houses painted white. In a small bar I asked whether they knew of any Fernandes Pretel family in town. A man, seated at a table, who was listening to my question, surprised that I, a foreigner, was speaking very good Spanish, answered, "Yes, I know a Fernandes Pretel family at Gracia Street." He showed me how to get there. It wasn't difficult to find the street and the number of the house.

I knocked at the house and a lady opened the door and welcomed me, smiling. When I said that I was looking for a Fernandes Pretel family she asked me to come in and said that maybe her uncle, who was sitting in the kitchen, might know some people who went to Brazil. He was a senior, advanced in age, who could not remember too much. I started a conversation with him and when I mentioned that my grandparents and my parents went by boat to Brazil and then were taken by train to "*la rueda de Jahu*" (the outskirts of the city of

Appendix

Jaú), São Paulo," he widened his eyes, as though he was looking into the past, remembering when he used to write letters to his family in Brazil, who had left his pueblo in Spain, looking for a better life in a distant land.

"Yes, I remember people of mine who left, but I never saw them again."

I thanked him and the lady who had answered the door and I left the house a little emotional about having the opportunity to visit that region of Andalucía, Spain, where my father's family came from.

I went up the hill, admiring those old small houses, full of history, written on walls that remain silent without telling us the main reason why so many people left to take the place of the slaves in a tropical land in South America.

Up on top of the hill on the main street of Jete I met Lucimar, Jack and Lois at the same place where I left them, on El Suspiro del Moro road, that crosses Jete from south to north, toward the city Granada. I took our car and drove slowly south to Almuñécar, on the tropical coast of Spain.

We arrived at the shore of the Mediterranean Sea. We found a restaurant facing a beach, which was almost deserted. It was May, still cold! We sat at a table and were served a free small plate of "paella," the typical food of Spain. We then ordered some drinks, spent some time talking about our trip to that part of Andalucía and then drove back to Marbella, west of Málaga, where we were staying.

My mother always said to us, in Brazilian Spanish, that she always remembered the Sierra Nevada, where there was snow all year round.

REV. JOÃO GARCIA

Bachelor of Theology from São Paulo Faculdade Teológica Batista
Studies at the Abbey Christian School for the English Language
Postgraduate studies at Spurgeon's College, London, England

He was ordained to the ministry at First Baptist Church, Curitiba, Paraná, Brazil, taught New Testament theology at the Curitiba Baptist Theological Seminary and was pastor of Prado Baptist Church, Curitba, Paraná, Brazil, and of First Baptist Church, Ponta Grossa, Paraná, Brazil.

In March 1979, he was accepted by the World Mission Board to be a missionary in Canada, in a project of the Baptist Convention of Ontario and Quebec and the Brazilian Baptist Convention to reach out into the Portuguese speaking communities of Ontario.

He and his family worked for thirty years taking the message of the gospel to those Portuguese people who have made Canada their new country.

He has also made several missionary trips to Cuba and the Azores, and he now writes devotionals for the periodical *Presente Diário* (*Daily Gift*), which is published in São Paulo, Brazil. He preaches in English, Portuguese and Spanish when invited by churches.

Hs is married to Lucimar Calvello Garcia. They have three children, Victor Manoel, Daniel Conrado and Marcos Raphael, all married, and have five granddaughters and three grandsons.

www.ingramcontent.com/pod-product-compliance
Lightning Source LLC
Chambersburg PA
CBHW071816080526
44589CB00012B/812